The Utopian Thought of
RESTIF de la BRETONNE

The Utopian Thought of
RESTIF de la BRETONNE

MARK POSTER
University of California, Irvine

New York: NEW YORK UNIVERSITY PRESS
1971

For Frank E. Manuel
with respect

Acknowledgments

To Professor Frank E. Manuel go my deepest thanks not only for assisting me through my fledgling steps in the preparation of this book, but especially for helping to form me as a historian of ideas. Professor Leo Gershoy read my manuscript and offered many clarifying suggestions. Professors Edward Tannenbaum and David Hicks also read parts of the manuscript. My friend, Professor Stanley Pacion provided me with an uncorruptible critic. Peter Remler deserves credit for many felicitous modifications of style. Thanks are also due to the librarians of the Bibliothèque Nationale and the Archives Nationale for their information about Restif's manuscripts; the librarians of Houghton Library of Harvard University, Columbia University, and the Public Library of New York City for making their collections available to me. Dr. Theodore Bestermann has graciously given me permission to use in this book my article, "The Concepts of Sexual Identity and Life Cycle in Restif's Utopian Thought," which appeared in *Studies on Voltaire and the Eighteenth Century*, LXXIII, 1970, 241–271. No married man writes a book without the encouragement and help of his wife. My wife, Marianne, suffered a burden beyond the normal oppression of women so that this book could be completed.

Contents

Editorial Note

All translations from the French are by the author except where the footnote indicates an English edition. All emphases in direct quotations are Restif's except where otherwise indicated.

The following is a list of abbreviations used in the footnotes. Restif's name has been omitted in all references to his writings. I have kept Restif's spelling since it was part of his project of reforms.

L'Andrographe for *L'Andrographe, ou Idées d'un honnête-homme sur un projet de règlement, proposé à toutes les nations de l'europe, pour opérer une réforme générale des moeurs, et par elle, le bonheur du genre humain* (Paris: Duchesne and Belin, 1782).

Les Contemporaines for *Les Contemporaines, ou Avantures des plus jolies femmes de l'âge présent* (Paris: Belin, 1780–1782), 17 vols.

La Découverte australe for *La Découverte australe par un homme volant ou, Le Dédale français* (Paris: n.p., 1781), 4 vols.

Les Gynographes for *Les Gynographes, ou Idées de deux honnêtes-femmes sur un projet de règlement proposé à toute l'Europe pour mettre les femmes à leur place, et opérer le bonheur des deux sexes* (Paris: Humblot, 1777).

Mes Inscriptions for *Mes Inscriptions*, ed. by P. Cottin (Paris: Bibliothèque Elzevirienne, 1889).

La Mimographe for *La Mimographe, ou Idées d'un honnête-femme pour la réformation du théâtre national* (Amsterdam: n.p., 1770)

Monsieur Nicolas, Pauvert edition for *Monsieur Nicolas, ou Le Coeur humain dévoilé* (Paris: Tuileries, 1959), 6 vols.

Monsieur Nicolas, Ellis edition for *Monsieur Nicolas*, ed. by Ellis, trans. by R. Mathers (London: Rodker, 1930), 6 vols.

Le Nouvel Abeilard for *Le Nouvel Abeilard, ou Lettres de deux amans qui ne se sont jamais vus* (Paris: Duchesne, 1778), 4 vols.

Le Nouvel Emile for *Le Nouvel Emile, ou L'Education pratique* (Paris: Costard, 1770–1776), 4 vols.

Le Nouvel Emile, Bachelin edition for *L'Oeuvre de Restif de la Bretonne*, ed. by H. Bachelin (Paris: Editions du Trianon, 1930–1932), Vol. 3.

Les Nuits de Paris for *Les Nuits de Paris, ou le Spectateur nocturne* (Paris: n.p., 1788–1794), 8 vols.

Les Nuits de Paris, Barzun edition for *Les Nuits de Paris*, ed. by Barzun, trans. by Asher and Fertig (New York: Random House, 1964).

Les Nuits de Paris, Boussel edition for *Les Nuits de Paris*, ed. by Boussel (Paris: Union générale d'éditions, 1963).

Le Palais Royal for *Le Palais Royal* (Paris: Guillot, 1790), 3 vols.

Le Paysan perverti for *Le Paysan perverti, ou les Dangers de la ville* (Bruxelles: Kistemaeckers, 1886), 2 vols.

Le Pornographe for *Le Pornographe, ou Idées d'un honnête-homme sur un projet de règlement pour les prostituées* (The Hague: Gosse and Pinet, 1770).

Les Posthumes for *Les Posthumes, Lettres reçues après la mort du Mari, par sa femme, qui le croit à Florence* (Paris: Duchesne, 1802), 4 vols.

Le Thesmographe for *Le Thesmographe, ou Idées d'un honnête-homme sur un projet de réglement, proposé à toutes les nations de l'Europe, pour opérer une réforme générale des loix* (Paris: Maradan, 1789).

La Vie de mon père for *La Vie de mon père*, ed. by Alméras (Paris: Michaud, n.d.).

PART I
Analysis of Utopian Values and Ideas

I

The Moralist and His Utopias

A. The Eccentric Owl

Nicolas Edme Restif de la Bretonne, the son of a Burgundian peasant proprietor, was born in 1734 in Sacy. He died in Paris in 1806. The years of his life were filled with turbulent love affairs and an enormous output of books. He was not a contemplative man, crouching in a poorly lit room in meditation over the nature of man and the universe. Restif lived completely in this world, draining the juices of earthly existence dry by an active, constant participation in the daily routines of Parisian life. If he was not a philosopher, neither was he a scholar. Although he acquired competence in several languages, he was not well schooled, spending only a few years in a Jansenist seminary. The ideas that we will be considering were not the result of painful study or erudition. Apart from the required reading of the seminary, a nodding acquaintance with Roman dramatists, and a knowledge of the novels he set in type as a printer, Restif's reading list was short. He was too fascinated by pretty girls and lower-class life to isolate himself from the pulsebeat of the Parisian streets in some dreary library. His life was hectic, tumultuous, passionate—and he wrote what he saw, felt, and imagined. The abstract constructs of reason had little significance for him except where they captured his experience and expressed his needs. Thus, when he won a chair in history at Moulins for a prize essay,[1] he declined entrance into the respectability and security of the academy, even though he was in financial straits, because he could not separate himself from the active life.

[1] This essay no longer exists. See F. Funck-Brentano, "Rétif de la Bretonne, professeur d'histoire à Moulins," *Revue des études historiques,* année 77 (1911), pp. 589–594.

Restif was a phenomenon in the intellectual and literary society of Paris: by birth a peasant, rude and vulgar; by trade a lowly printer; by vocation an artist who had the audacity to write novels, novels that appeared faster than one could read them, that expressed passions so strong that they shocked polite sensibility, that were written with a monstrous lack of form and concerned the least distinguished actions of humanity. Restif walked the streets of Paris at night in search of literary subject matter, calling himself an owl and wearing a cape that was tattered with age and would have been out of fashion in the most inconspicuous provincial hamlet. And this man deemed himself a worthy subject for an autobiography that filled nineteen volumes. To further bewilder his contemporaries, this barely educated, half-savage peasant wrote treatises on sublime, abstract subjects like morality and natural philosophy. Most brazen of all were Restif's utopian projects. He took upon himself nothing less than the total reform of society. It is thus the utopian thought of a unique man that will be the topic of this study.

B. The Dilemma of the Moralist

To Restif, utopia was a nowhere that juxtaposed alternatives to an imperfect reality. His deep-seated wishes were embodied in visions of an ideal society and they reflected his displeasure with the conduct of his contemporaries. Since eighteenth-century thought was dominated by a search for a principle of morality, for an ethic that could guide man toward happiness, it was natural for Restif to cast his image of the perfect society in moral terms. In his utopian writings he confronted the task of reforming France and creating a new moral world.

The broad lines of inquiry and the basic premises of a new ethical doctrine had been defined for Restif earlier in the century by materialists, sensationalists, and utilitarians. La Mettrie, Condillac, Helvétius, and d'Holbach had propounded a new view of man. The universe consisted of matter alone; man was related to the outer world by the sensations he received from it; these were of two kinds, pleasure and pain; the former was good and the latter bad; virtue consisted of maximizing pleasure and minimizing pain; happiness, identical with virtue, was a technique of manipulating the environment to procure the utmost utility, or the greatest favorable balance of pleasure over pain; by attaining this personal happiness one did, at the same time, achieve the greatest good for society. In its barest and most simplified outline, this was the point of departure for Restif's ethical doctrine.

The neat boundaries of this sensationalist theory were broken through by the jagged edges of Restif's thought. For Condillac and the others, nature provided an even flow of sensations that constituted information, telling man about the outside world. Man used reason to sort out the data and acted on the principle of maximum pleasure. The role given to reason by the philosophes, and their notion of the identity of sensation and knowledge were not taken over by Restif. The stimuli of the external world were related, for him, not to the sorting-machine brain, but to the feelings, the passions. Placing himself beside Rousseau and the sentimental school of novelists, Restif saw sensations only in terms of subjective pleasure and pain. The fact of overwhelming importance to him was that man could feel pleasure and pain—not that these sensations related man to the universe and provided the groundwork for an empirical theory of knowledge or for science. Restif's "science" was not one of objectivity toward nature; it was the science of the human heart.[2] Moral science meant understanding one's own feelings; nature was revealed by intro-spection, not by performing experiments in the material world. The philosophes had expounded a doctrine of sensationalism with a view toward fixing man's place in nature so that God's assistance would be unnecessary. Revelation was an obsolete form of knowledge because man could experience the world directly. By the 1780's interests had shifted. Following Rousseau, Restif was repulsed by the mechanistic philosophy; after the retreat from God to the physical world, the time had come to withdraw from the physical world to the intimacy of the individual and his feelings.[3]

Many thinkers had already recognized the role of feeling in moral theory. Primarily in England, with only faint echoes in France, theorists from Shaftesbury to Adam Smith had sought the basis of morality in sympathy toward others, a natural feeling of benevolence. They had re-jected the hard-headed self-interest theory of d'Holbach in favor of a more sociable doctrine: man had an innate sense of altruism for his fellows. Restif found the theory of moral sentiment no more convincing than the egoism of d'Holbach. In fact, to him, only self-interest afforded a realistic basis for moral conduct. "It is necessary to give morality a general base which is more or less solid: this base is personal interest." [4] Restif argued with the sensationalists and against the sentimentalists, but he changed the grounds of the morality of self-interest. Not only did he conceive of man as a feeling animal, thereby rendering sensationalism subjective, but he gave a unique interpretation to the nature of these feelings.

[2] *Le Thesmographe*, p. 396.
[3] *Monsieur Nicolas*, Pauvert edition, VI, 224.
[4] *Ibid.*, VI, 104.

According to Restif, there was a constant war in man's heart between opposing feelings. Nature consisted of opposites: [5] pleasure and pain, good and evil were all essential facts of the human condition. "I have perhaps not insisted enough on the necessity of pleasure and of sadness in the physical realm, and of vice and virtue in the moral in order for a full, entire existence of sensibility." [6] But the fullness of life was only possible when "extreme pleasure and extreme sadness" were felt: only then would man be "perfect." [7] Restif's favorite human examples of these opposite principles of nature were Fénelon and Sade; both principles were necessary for freedom. [8] With this emphasis on the polarity of nature and the idea that life, or reality, was to be found at the dialectical extremes of experience, Restif shattered the normative tone of moderation of the eighteenth century.

Restif likened himself to Epicurus for recognizing the full force of a morality of pleasure (volupté). [9] He compared his war on all forms of puritanism, especially the Jansenist variety under which he was educated, to the battle between the Epicureans and the Stoics. [10] To follow the Stoics—to deny one's feelings, to renounce sensibility for a life of even, gray tones, to give up the deep intensity of pleasure—was inhuman.

A man is tortured and does not cry out. What does that prove? That he suffers less than another, or is a better man? Not at all: but only that his fiber . . . is stronger. Does this tougher fiber, which is so admired, make him a better son, a better husband, a better father or a better friend? No. It makes him hard and difficult . . . to live with . . . the real man cries out or retaliates when he is hit. . . . The stoic denatures man. . . . [11]

Hence the new morality consisted in the full acceptance of man's sentient capacity. Yet if the nature of the human heart were a polar struggle between the extremes of pleasure and pain, good and evil, and the moral man were one who felt this struggle most deeply, would not the moral man, besides being as good as Fénelon, be as evil as Sade? Was it humanly possible to give free expression to one's feelings and remain in society? This was the basic question that Restif discovered and felt constrained to answer. Given the full life of the passions, reason was of no avail; no one

[5] *Ibid.*, VI, 119.
[6] *Ibid.*, V, 450.
[7] *Ibid.*, V, 451.
[8] *Ibid.*, V, 450.
[9] *Ibid.*, V, 476.
[10] *Ibid.*
[11] *Monsieur Nicolas*, Ellis edition, I, 92.

could—or should—control his feelings. How was any society possible, much less utopia, if man were helplessly enthralled in a dialectic of pleasures and pains? Addressing himself to these questions, Restif drew out the full implications of sensationalist psychology. If benevolence, conscience, and remorse were all denied, if reason were seen as a weak tool incapable of directing action, and finally, if man were a creature open only to sensations, how were kindness, justice, and virtue possible?

As Restif saw it, there was really no way to make the individual moral. To be moral meant to do unto others as you would have them do unto you; it meant to deal justly with one's fellows. But the strongest motivations—self-interest and the passions—both militated against consideration for others. Self-interest was not in harmony with the common interest, while the passions of benevolence and sympathy were weak. The only possible answer was reason; reason to restrain self-interest in light of the needs of society and reason to control the passions and render man sociable, if not altruistic. But Restif did not believe that reason was strong enough to accomplish these ends.

Since it was foolhardy to count on the individual's capacity to act morally toward his fellows, the path to morality had to lead through the collectivity or society. Only the group was strong enough to coerce the individual into moral behavior. Utopia, then, would be the perfect arrangement of social institutions and controls.

Restif's reliance on society to make individuals moral was typical of his age.[12] Rousseau's *Contrat social* was the first clear expression of this postulate, placing the general will high above each individual as the vehicle of collective morality. The *Contrat social* was an early statement of the modern dilemma of the tension between individual and society. Restif was in agreement with Rousseau, his acknowledged mentor. Society had to be given overwhelming authority in face of the impossibility of individual moral behavior. The only way to avoid complete tyranny was to find a legislator equal to the legendary Lycurgus one who could establish laws that without being arbitrary, would restrain the individual for society's benefit.

Overtly, Restif was a social utilitarian. "The base of morality is common reciprocal utility. . . . the most efficacious means of having personal happiness is to work for general happiness." [13] He differed from Helvétius and other social utilitarians in two respects: (1) he saw no possibility of a natural harmony of interest between individuals, and (2) his emphasis on the passions and the specifically volatile quality he gave them

[12] Lester Crocker, *Nature and Culture* (Baltimore: Johns Hopkins, 1963), p. 396.
[13] *Monsieur Nicolas,* Pauvert edition, VI, 37.

made the easy moral conditioning of the individual impossible. In short, he faced the moral problem in particularly acute terms and envisioned no cure short of drastically reordering society.

Personal interest, which is a spontaneous plant, always grows with a force double that of social interest, a delicate, artificial plant, which needs great tending to thrive. We have only one way to correct personal interest and compel it to contribute to the social good: that is to graft it onto the general interest. But how to make this graft? By completely changing our present regime; by tightening the ties of society; by discarding all that isolates us and separates our interests. . . .[14]

Virtue was thus "the victory of the general interest against the particular interest." [15] Not only must the individual's interest be subordinated to the social good, but, due to the turbulence of man's passions, the act of social "grafting" had to be especially severe. The projects designed to achieve the golden rule foretold a rigorous repression of individual whim. Men were inherently vicious toward their fellows: the explosive passions introduced a principle of evil that had to be restrained. "Since the human species has an extreme sensibility . . . it serves him in tormenting his brothers and making them suffer. . . ." [16] The utopian who began by identifying himself with Epicurus and the celebration of the passions ended by doing battle on the side of the puritans. This paradox runs deep in Restif's thought.

Restif's social utilitarianism was therefore a unique moral theory. His focus was always on how to transform man into a social being, that is, to make him moral. But he began with an image of man as an explosively passionate creature and he accepted—or rather, affirmed—man's passions as the key to all pleasure. Thus, at the core of Restif's thought there was a split, a division, and its recognition is crucial to any understanding of his utopianism. To Restif the social utilitarian, happiness was conceivable only in a moral community that created order and security—the very premises of happiness. To Restif the Epicurean, happiness was to be found only in the gratification of the passions and this often led to one's happiness only at the cost of another's misery. Thus happiness required the working out of opposing values: austere moralism and sensual Epicureanism; an orderly, secure concept of society and a vivacious, turbulent view of man; a profound respect for justice among men and a fundamental affirmation of the unjust, even cruel passions. This tenuous equi-

[14] *Ibid.*, VI, 39.
[15] *Ibid.*, VI, 50.
[16] *La Découverte australe*, IV, 31.

librium between id and superego was the central element in Restif's utopian thought. At times unable to maintain the precarious balance, he asserted positions so completely at odds with one another that the reader, in bewildered amazement, is tempted to write him off as hopelessly confused. Yet he embodied and attempted to resolve tendencies that were deeply engrained in the thought of his time, and for this he deserves a place in the history of utopian thought. Anyone who articulates both the repressive demands of civilization on man and the primary needs of the individual's instinctive nature warrants our examination.

C. The Documents

The first task of this study is to establish the pertinent documents. What were the utopias of Restif de la Bretonne and in which of his works can they be found? The question is not a simple one because throughout his works, whatever their genre, he described plans or rules for the establishment of an ideal society. In the eighteenth century, only Abbé Saint-Pierre approached Restif in the extent of consideration given to utopian projects. If Restif wrote two hundred volumes of fiction about the relations of the sexes, he always kept an eye open for a clue, a hint, or a glimpse of the path to utopia.

A review of his utopian writings reveals that they are not all of equal significance. Some were mere fragments, no longer than a page or two; others took several volumes to complete. I shall outline in chronological order the great majority of his utopias, indicating those I consider most relevant to this study, and those containing his ideas in their clearest and most comprehensive expression. While mapping out Restif's utopias one must consider the authenticity of the atuhorship, for some of his have been attributed to other writers, while a few works by others have been wrongly attributed to Restif.

The earliest of Restif's utopias was the first volume in a series called *Idées singulières*, which was published in 1769, just two years after his first novel. The *Idées singulières* consisted of the following books:

> *Le Pornographe,* 1769
> *La Mimographe,* 1770
> *Les Gynographes,* 1777
> *L'Andrographe,* 1782
> *Le Thesmographe,* 1789
> *Le Glossographe,* 1796–1797
> (a fragment included in *Monsieur Nicolas*)

The *Idées singulières* was Restif's most ambitious utopian work and it will be the major source for this study. In these volumes he set forth an architectonic system of laws for the reform of society. There was another volume that he sometimes included in the *Idées singulières:* volume four of *Le Nouvel Emile,* which appeared in 1770, had the title *L'Educographe.* It amounted to 48 pages of an introduction for the full work. On page 45 he began the utopia, but stopped, referring the reader to his future book *L'Andrographe.* *Le Nouvel Emile* was revised to meet the censor's demands and published as *L'Ecole des pères* in 1776, but *L'Educographe* was not included. There is thus no reason to list *L'Educographe* among the *Idées singulières.*

The titles of these volumes are of some interest. The nouns were taken from Greek stems and denote "the reformer of ———": the reformer of prostitution is *le pornographe,* the reformer of the theater is *la mimographe,* of women is *le gynographe,* of men is *l'andrographe,* of laws is *le thesmographe,* and of language is *le glossographe.* Except for the last, they all appeared in the form of letters, frequently interspersed with short stories to elucidate the thesis of the reforms. The bulk of each volume was a series of regulations, often followed by supposed objections from readers and answers by Restif. The style is monotonous and laborious to read, in sharp contrast to many of Restif's other works. After the regulations comes a series of notes labeled part two of each book. These are quite extraordinary pieces and they indicate Restif's encyclopedic bent and his disorganized temperament. The *Notes historiques et justificatives* are primarily reviews of the customs of the whole world, based on travel reports relating to the topic under consideration. Thus, in *Les Gynographes* are described practices relating to women, especially marriage customs, from China to Tahiti. Among the notes are also essays on topics like happiness and love: some were not written by Restif at all, but this is normally quite obvious to the reader since his style is unique. As the reader proceeds he discovers a play or two or some little story that Restif could not fit in anywhere else. Especially in *Le Thesmographe,* Restif's organization was weak.

Le Pornographe and *La Mimographe* were devoted to specific institutions and were not integrated into the larger utopian vision. They form a subseries in the *Idées singulières* and will be dealt with briefly in this study. Restif's central utopian works were *Les Gynographes* and *L'Andrographe.* They were intricately cross-referenced and they form a totality with a clearly enunciated and fairly consistent framework of ideas. When in writing other works Restif was reminded of social abuses, it was *Les Gynographes* and *L'Andrographe* that he recommended to his readers as antidotes to the existing ills. *Le Thesmographe* was dated 1789, but it did not appear until 1790.[17] In a prefatory letter, Restif dedicated the book to the Estates General, hoping they would consummate the revolution by instituting his projects. The book was aimed directly at the current political situation, and was couched in a softer, more attractive tone than *Les Gynographes* and *L'Andrographe*. Restif was excited by the prospect that the moment of realization had come for his visionary ideas. But laws and political institutions were not his forte and he took several opportunities in *Le Thesmographe* to recommend the earlier two books as the intellectual foundation of the New France. Accordingly, *Le Thesmographe* will have somewhat less emphasis in this study. Too much of it is devoted to dietribes against lawyers, a group with which Restif had much trouble during his lifetime. Finally, the fragment *Le Glossographe*, containing some interesting ideas and some that were far-fetched and bizarre, will not be considered. Here Restif tried to make French spelling phonetic, to "purify" prefixes and suffixes by following Latin and Greek more strictly, and to formulate a more "efficient" alphabet.

The bibliophile Lacroix[18] made several arbitrary guesses about the authorship of the *Idées singulières* since he could not conceive of Restif's writing these books alone. According to Lacroix, *Le Pornographe* was partly the work of Linguet, *La Mimographe* received Nougaret's aid, and Ginguiné, Linguet, and Butel-Dumont all helped Restif with *Le Thesmographe*. To varying degrees these men were all acquaintances of Restif. Lacroix's irresponsibility becomes apparent when he goes on to attribute other works to Restif which allegedly he was able to accomplish by himself but for his authorship of which there is not a shred of proof, and to claim that the "graphes" were published under Restif's name only to take responsibility off the respectable shoulders of Linguet and the others. *La Philosophie du Ruvarebohni* and *Catéchisme social, ou exposition familière*, published together in Paris by Le Normant in 1808 (two years after Restif's death), signed by "P.J.J.S.** et Nicolas Bugnet" and "Nicolas Bugnet" respectively, and bearing none of the unique spellings or printing marks of Restif, were, according to Lacroix, Restif's own books. These works contain many interesting ideas but they bear no resemblance to those of Restif. The *Catéchisme* contains a statement of the inheritance of acquired characteristics that was completely

[17] Adolphe Tabarant, *Le Vrai visage de Restif de la Bretonne* (Paris: Editions Montaigne, 1936), p. 272.

[18] Paul Lacroix, *Bibliographie et iconographie de tous les ouvrages de Restif de la Bretonne* (Paris: Fontaine, 1875), p. 321.

alien to Restif's thought.[19] It is enough to note that the excellent bibliography by J. Rives Childs does not include these works and gives Restif full credit for the *Idées singulières*.

The *Idées singulières* were not popular works, and only *Le Pornographe* received more than one edition. Restif put out a second edition in 1776 and a critical edition appeared in 1879. The book was also translated into German and Italian.

Restiff also expressed his utopian ideas in his novels. *Le Paysan perverti, ou Les Dangers de la ville* (1776) contains a short series of regulations entitled "Statuts du Bourg d'Oudun" tacked on the end of the last volume. These were intended to turn a village into a utopian community. *L'Ecole des pères* (1776) contains a three-page version of the same idea.[20] *Le Nouvel Abeilard* includes a model series of laws for four urban couples,[21] with a story relating the success of the enterprise. The forty-two-volume *Les Contemporaines* continues the series of plans: *Les 20 épouses des 20 associés, Nouveau moyen de bannir l'ennui du ménage* (1780) is a utopia for artisans in Paris.[22]

At this point Restif wrote another major utopian work, this time devoting an entire novel to it. *La Découverte australe par un homme volant, ou Le Dédale français* (1781) in four volumes, was begun during a severe illness[23] and reflected the physical restrictions of the author by its extravagant flights of fantasy, perhaps the most bizarre book to appear in the century. Taking Cyrano de Bergerac's *Le Voyage dans la lune* (1657) as his model, Restif escaped the confinements of the sick bed through the adventures of his hero, Victorin, in Australia. This conglomeration of novel and scientific essay depicted a number of utopias: le mont inaccessible in France, l'isle Christine, l'isle Victorin and Megapatagonia in Australia. The last is the most noteworthy and truly utopian of these ideal societies. The story begins with the invention of a flying machine that is a credit to Restif's Leonardesque imagina-

---

[19] Nicolas Bugnet, *Catéchisme social, ou Exposition familière* (Paris: Le Normant, 1808), p. 49. A definitive disclaimer of Restif's authorship may be found in an anonymous article, "Une Utopie rare, L'Utopie de Ruvarebohni," *Bulletin of the International Institute for Social History* (Amsterdam, 1937), No. 1, pp. 26–35. The two works were mistakenly attributed to Restif, following Lacroix, by Hugo Lindemann (Stuttgart-Degerloch) in "Restif de la Bretonne," *Archiv für die Geschichte des Sozialismus und der Arbeiterbewegung*, ed. by Carl Grunberg, No. 3 (1913), pp. 211–275.

[20] III, 370–372.

[21] III, 336–408.

[22] II, 389–455.

[23] *Monsieur Nicolas*, Pauvert edition, VI, 586–587.

tion. An umbrella-like instrument, the invention was designed to be pedal-operated so as to leave the arms free. Three years later the Montgolfier brothers shocked France with their experiments with flight. There was more to the adventures of "the French Daedalus" than a mere mechanical invention, however, for Victorin discovered creatures that illustrated Restif's thesis of the variety of the human species. In Australia he found "the Man-dog," "the Man-elephant," "the Man-ape," "the Man-sheep," "the Man-goat," and many other strange animals, all demonstrating that man is as diverse as other animal species in biological constitution. Finally, Volume IV, the "Lettre d'un singe," was a scathing attack on the human race by a monkey. The monkey was born of a human female and a baboon.

Restif's attempt at journalism, Les Nuits de Paris, ou Le Spectateur nocturne, contained a table of laws for thirty Parisian families.[24] Monsieur Nicolas (1797) capped the Idées singulières with a few final regulations,[25] stimulated by the events of the Revolution. The last utopia of importance came in Les Posthumes: Plan d'une liberté absolue pour les Français Républicains.[26] The small utopias or "plans of association," contain similar ideas. The most representative, Statuts du Bourg d'Oudun and Les 20 épouses des 20 associés, will be given some consideration and the rest will be omitted from the discussion.

Hence this study will concentrate on three works: Les Gynographes (1777), La Découverte australe par un homme volant (1781), and L'Andrographe (1782). They contain the core of Restif's vision. Furthermore, they appeared within a five-year period, and thus suggest a topical treatment rather than a chronological approach which is, at any rate, unnecessary in a study of Restif's utopias since his basic ideas remained more or less constant over the entire period of his writing (1767 to 1802). The study is divided into two parts. In the first, each chapter deals with an idea or a cluster of ideas that forms a coherent whole in itself. The task of fixing Restif's position in the thought of the century has not yet been adequately done and it is hoped that these chapters will accomplish that end. The last three chapters deal with Restif's utopian thought as a whole and attempt to interpret it from the different perspectives of psychology, sociology, and the utopian tradition. Like most scholars of Restif's thought, I have found it impossible to set rigid boundaries between his life and his ideas, and a preference for the theory of psychological determinants must be avowed. Restif was a

---

[24] 1790 edition, V, 966–968.
[25] Monsieur Nicolas, Pauvert edition, VI, 312–325, 376–381.
[26] IV, 128–133.

printer by trade and would often set his own type. In fact, he sometimes wrote directly into type without any manuscript; although his haste often rendered his thought confused, contradictory, and obscure, it nonetheless allowed an unusual directness of expression. Restif worked with passion and his passions worked powerfully in his thought. His writings also reveal a forceful if eccentric personality, bent on self-expression and heedless of models and general opinion. Confirmation of his fiery individuality is evident in the reactions of contemporaries to his writings. Whether the judgment of Restif was favorable or not, most of his readers in the eighteenth century saw him as an "original."

II

Education

A. PARIS, SACY, AND SEXUAL IDENTITY

Restif's observations of the mores of Paris led him to the conclusion that something was drastically wrong with society. Some cancerous cell, deeply embedded in Parisian customs, was eating away at the marrow of the social body, causing all manner of disorders. The moralist set out to unveil the sickness and prescribe a cure before the patient died, before this principle of disorder spread and society degenerated into anarchy. The diagnosis Restif made suggested the direction of the remedy. While the philosophes harangued social authorities for failing to modernize feudal conventions and for not limiting the obnoxious power of the Church, Restif gave a new turn to social criticism. The trouble with society was not too little enlightenment; it was a disorder in the organization of the passions.

To Restif the passions were the crucial factor in the relations of men in society. The passions were manifest in all social interactions and if society did not provide for their proper expression, disorder would ensue. The particular failing of France was the tendency of sexual roles to become confused, blurred, and even crossed in the freedom of city life. Nowhere did Restif attempt a sustained analysis of the social phenomenon he called the "equalization" of the sexes. Instead, at various points in his novels and utopian works, he sounded a cry of despair over the behavior of his contemporaries. "The two sexes have essentially different constitutions and they must be raised in almost totally opposite ways. One of the most dangerous abuses of present education is the desire to establish a parity between them." [1]

[1] *L'Andrographe*, p. 71.

15

Restif saw clothing styles as a barometer of this immoral pattern of Parisian manners. Fancy, soft, wigged, and perfumed—how unmanly the rococo male seemed to him!

. . . if one examines the people who are attempting to intermingle the two sexes, one will find that they are vicious individuals. The woman with a man's hat, with breeches, has a hard, imperious, unlovable, unsocial character. The man with pointed shoes is a fop, effeminate, a trifler, and often worse still, a pederast! [2]

The identification Restif made between outward appearance and moral stature was not untypical of the eighteenth-century moralist. What was unusual about the nature of Restif's complaint was that this immorality was attributed to a lack of sexual identity. He denounced as immoral clothing styles "which brought together the adornment of the two sexes." [3] This "proto-Balzacian" novelist, who called himself a "spectator" and whose novels are extolled for their realism, observed French society toward the end of the Old Regime with great accuracy and fidelity to the truth.

One of his graphic cameos from Les Nuits de Paris, called "Le Garçon en fille," captures the moralist's point with vivid reality.

At the corner of rue Champ-Fleuri I saw a small gathering of people; I approached them. There stood what seemed to be a girl of about sixteen, whose sweet demeanor they were admiring. I was struck by her gentle, innocent beauty. I spoke to her, asking how she had drawn this attention to her. She smiled at me, and nothing in the world was so enchanting as her smile. I was puzzled until, without a word, the child raised her skirts and exhibited her breeches. Then I understood that this was a boy, who was amusing himself in a scarcely suitable fashion. . . . I draw a veil over the rest of this horrid tale. Suffice it to say that this child is an effeminate today. . . . [4]

Restif attacked this society not because it was Christian, the bane of the philosophes—or untraditional, which betokened evil to the Christian writers—but because it eroded the enjoyment of pleasure. The melting of the sexual line thwarted sensuality; only when each sex fulfilled its role could each attract and please the other. This became the basis for his critique of Parisian mores.

On his father's farm, La Bretonne, one's role and personality were largely determined at birth through the accident of sex. A boy knew that the management of affairs and the leadership of the family would

[2] Monsieur Nicholas, Pauvert edition, VI, 451–452.
[3] Ibid., VI, 450–451.
[4] Les Nuits de Paris, Barzun edition, pp. 30–31.

someday be his; little girls expected to face the duties of keeping house. The patriarchal style of life made inexorable demands on character development. Conformity was a must and deviations from time-honored patterns were punished by dreaded social exclusion and the whispering condemnation of village gossip. A peasant's education provided a clear sense of identity with one's sex. Such were the inbred standards and unconscious assumptions Restif carried with him to Paris. With this baggage he confronted the refined effeminacy of rococo men and the imperious manners of salon women. The strange, complex personalities of Paris threatened the very basis of his world image:

Look at the disorder and the kind of anarchy which reigns nowadays in civil society. One would wish that the European nations took effective measures to bring harmony back to the heart of families, giving to those who are the natural chiefs the authority that has been usurped by women, into whose hands it is so visibly displaced that the usurpation makes women and men equally unhappy.[5]

He saw the world as upside down and he took upon himself the job of turning it right side up.

B. Nature

Restif's notion of reordering society by educating in terms of sexual identitiy fell within a long tradition of Western thought. That men and women should not express their peculiar, individual capacities, but rather those of their sex, was a moral teaching of the Bible and a symbolic teaching of ancient cosmogonies. Jansenism, relying heavily on the Old Testament, resurrected a Judaic, patriarchal family model. In the Hebrew tradition, man and woman had distinct functions to perform that required distinct attributes of character. Besides Christian and Jewish traditions, there were the mythic descriptions of the origin of the universe, in which masculine and feminine forces or gods provided the basis for a primitive cosmogony. At the dawn of human society, the family was legitimated by myth. In Hesiod's *Theogony*, the evolution of the cosmos and the story of the Greek pantheon were described in terms of a struggle between Mother Earth, the feminine principle, and Zeus, the masculine principle.[6] The same anthropomorphism is found in Egyptian and Chinese myths.

[5] *Les Gynographes*, p. 62.
[6] Norman O. Brown, introduction to Hesiod, *Theogony* (New York: Library of the Liberal Arts, 1953), p. 17.

These ancient conceptions of the origin of the universe through an interplay of male and female gods or primal forces are directly relevant to Restif's thought. Since sexual identity was corrupted in civilized Paris, it was necessary to return to nature for a reorganizing principle. Hence Restif invented a cosmogony similar to the Greek, Egyptian, and Chinese, and made it the religion of his utopians. He studied the religions of these ancient civilizations in a French translation of Bernstorf's *Atlas des religions*, which treated the primitive conceptions with some respect. In *La Découverte australe par un homme volant*, and again in a utopian section of *Monsieur Nicolas*, Restif outlined a scheme of the universe in terms of two great forces: the male and the female. The light his cosmogony casts on his idea of sexual identity may be seen in the specific roles he gave to each cosmic principle. Utopia is inconceivable until the human race harmonizes its nature with the male and female cosmic forces. As in the Chinese cosmogony, the male is the active principle and the female is the passive principle.[7] But unlike the Yin and the Yang, Restif's forces are complete opposites; no trace of femininity taints the masculine principle and vice versa. We shall see that Restif carried this extreme polarity into his educational ideal—men and women are as different as flowers and bees.

As with flowers and bees, however, it is the interaction of the male and the female that sustains life in the cosmos. Restif likened the male to the sun and the female to the planets: their "copulation" produces life.[8] Opposing Buffon, he guessed that the planets were never parts of the sun, separated during an accidental explosion, but comets, which entered into an orbit around the sun and were bombarded for millennia by the sun's "semen" or light. Thus, the planets became "fertilized" and life was born. Unlike Buffon's mechanistic description of the formation of the galaxy, Restif's had an organic cast: the sun gave birth to the planets. Part of this concept of the formation of the earth Restif took from a contemporary scientific theorist, Benoit de Maillet,[9] especially in *Telliamed, ou Entretiens d'un philosophe indien avec une missionaire français sur la démunition de la mer, la formation de la terre, l'origine de l'homme* (1748).[10] However, Restif did not rest with the intuitive version of creation given by De Maillet. Investing physical forces with sexual overtones was Restif's singular accomplishment. The bizarre image of the universe as an enormous field of copulating bodies was, no

[7] *Monsieur Nicolas*, Pauvert edition, V, 469.
[8] *Ibid.*, V, 63.
[9] *Ibid.*, V, 428.
[10] (London: Osborn).

doubt, a projection of his powerful erotic drives.[11] With this vision Restif provided a justification for a utopia that was based on nature, while grounding his thought in mythological tradition. Restif was aware that his likening the material cosmos to "a large animal" [12] was opposed to the Deists' clock image. He conceded that his own theory was based on an analogy, but he rejected the cosmogony of the philosophes because he found it absurd. His own had the advantage of poetic beauty.

I am well aware that . . . Baron d'Holbach . . . has pretended to prove, and has proven to certain misguided minds, that everything is due to chance. . . . How does he know it? Why prefer absurdity without proofs, to the beautiful analogies that I have exposed, that everyone supports, and that the ancient traditions and the Bible itself maintain? [13]

Restif's cosmogany was the natural law upon which his utopia rested, and as such it is significant. If his ruminations cannot be taken seriously as science, they least point up the quality of his thought. His concept of sexual identity was based securely enough on traditional Christian thought and ancient mythology, but it was given an impress all his own. The ideal types of masculinity and femininity were given the primacy of biological forces: the basis of utopian education was a reordering of instinctual energies. Men and women were slaves to the purpose of the human race, and destiny commanded that they carry out their biological functions. All of life was at stake in this vitalist conception. To understand why Restif was so vehemently opposed to the blurring of sexual roles in Paris, one must imagine what would happen, in the context of his cosmogony, if the sun suddenly stopped emitting its life-giving light and took on a female trait of receptivity. Chaos, disorder, anarchy—this is what Restif feared for France.

C. The Models

At the heart of Restif's utopian system of education were the models of masculinity and femininity. Education was the means of character formation, of imprinting a pattern on the personality of each child, and the syllabus consisted in the ideal types that Restif elaborated for each sex. Such a project involves several questions: What is the content of each ideal type? What are the methods of instruction? How does his system compare with others of his time, specifically, with Rousseau's?

[11] *Monsieur Nicolas*, Pauvert edition, V, 228.
[12] *Ibid.*, V, 277.
[13] *Ibid.*, V, 281.

In a definitive but unsystematic way, Restif outlined the male and the female patterns of utopian education. The male ideal was based on the cosmic-biological role of masculinity; man was the fertilizing being (*l'être fécondateur*).[14] The behavior of the male principle in the sexual act, the most natural and the most necessary act of man, provided the foundation for establishing the male personality and the male social role. Since man was the fertilizing being, he had to be educated to fulfill his function, not just biologically but culturally as well. Nature, in giving man an active role in the love act, intended that man must take the active role in building and guarding culture. "Destined by nature to act vigorously, to command, man has a role in the reproduction of the species which neither restrains nor subjugates him." [15] Restif intuitively grasped the idea later associated with Freudian and Jungian psychology that male consciousness is ego consciousness, and that civilization is masculine in the sense that it depends on the ability of the ego to pursue goals that are distant in time.[16] He phrased this idea in terms of the masculine heroic and active will: ". . . the temper of men's spirit makes them alone capable of great deeds. . . . It is only natural that man, who is the most vigorous and the most free, would be responsible for the weightier work; business which requires travels and long application. . . ." [17]

Femininity is the antithesis of masculinity; woman is the fertilized being (*l'être féconde*).[18] Her role in the sexual act is receptive and passive. Starting with the essential passivity of the feminine nature, Restif outlined the personality structure and social role of the woman. "What must we form in a woman? A being essentially agreeable: this is the clue as it includes utility, sweetness, submission, etc. Here is what all the Gynogogues [educators of women] must continually keep in mind. 'To please is the lot of women.' " [19] The concept of the pleasure-giving capacity is basic to the Restivian psychology of women. Again, the analogy with the Freudian and Jungian schools is appropriate; the female represents Eros, the more instinctual and the less self-conscious of the two ideal types. *Femme féïque* (fairy-like or enchanting) is the phrase he invented to express the feminine capacity to please, to mystify, and to attract. Just as masculinity indicates a capacity of the will, so feminity indicates a primarily sensuous and emotive capacity.

[14] *L'Andrographe*, p. 6.
[15] *Ibid.*
[16] See Erich Neumann, *The Origins and History of Consciousness*, trans. by R. Hull (New York: Harper Torchbook, 1962), II, 340.
[17] *Les Gynographes*, p. 58.
[18] *L'Andrographe*, p. 6.
[19] *Les Gynographes*, p. 36.

Women are "delicate" and unfit for heavy, brutal work; they are naturally constituted for doing the little things that make men happy.[20] Besides, females have no constancy and it would be folly to set them to long projects. A man is active; his will is "full, entire, firm"; a woman's actions are all "relative" and "conditional." "Man wills because he wills; woman never wills except by opposition or by imitation." [21]

At bottom both of Restif's ideal types contain polar antitheses. On the one hand he affirms the passions in each sex; on the other he calls for their renunciation. In the *Idées singulières*, women have to be the diffident companions, inferior in status to the patriarchal male. "The moral destiny of the woman is submission, economy, love of order, of occupation and the sedentary life." [22] A plain peasant woman chained to the routine of the farm is the image evoked here, an image that is the converse of the haughty, luxurious *dames* of Paris. No alluring adornments, just the unaltered plainness of nature is the style he demands. "How fair a thing is the instinctive decency of a girl who covers herself with modesty, as with a veil! It is the very enchantment of nature." [23] On the other hand, enchantment has another, more sensual quality and the utopian woman has an opposite side to her personality. It is incorrect to picture girls being educated only for housework. One should also conjure up an image of the alluring femininity of Restif's dream. At the opposite end of the earth from Paris, Restif's "flying man" discovered ideal femininity in Australia. There, women

practice among themselves seeing who can assume the most seductive smile, who will find the most effective means of pleasing men in all possible situations. For the idea is inculcated into them from childhood that they are made for man. . . .[24]

The masculine ideal is equally polarized: the young, dashing hero and the stern adult patriarch are both elements of Restif's utopian male. As with the women the contradiction is one of appearance because the hero and the patriarch are both needed to build and maintain utopia; sensual and devoted women are needed to capture a man and maintain his household. Both polarities arise from a deep ambivalence in Restif's thought: the passions are double-pronged. He glorifies them and calls for an end

[20] *Ibid.*, pp. 58–59.
[21] *L'Andrographe*, p. 7.
[22] *Les Gynographes*, p. 208.
[23] *Monsieur Nicolas*, Ellis edition, II, 89.
[24] *La Découverte australe*, III, 502–503, trans. by Frank and Fritzie Manuel in *French Utopias* (New York: Free Press, 1966), p. 171.

to Christian renunciation. Therefore the women should be titillating and the men heroic lovers. But he is equally aware of their dangers and he proposes a new set of repressions: hence the patriarch and his unstimulating wife.

D. The Method

To guarantee the education of the models he outlined, Restif enumerated in great detail the rules for rearing boys and girls. It is not necessary for us to explore at length the numerous prescriptions he laid out. Suffice it to say that they covered the full gamut of the life of the child. Swaddling, weaning, clothing, diet, hours of sleep, school curriculum, games, and all conceivable facets of childhood development were scrupulously discussed in the utopian's handbooks.

Some of Restif's educational ideas paralleled the main tendency of the century—the elimination of worn out, useless traditions. Utopian education was to be secular and the state must administer it. Also, the curriculum, which was not one of his central concerns, tended to show the influence of the Enlightenment: practical, secular, and scientific subjects took up a good portion of the course of study. In treating the more profound aspects of character formation, however, he fell away from the liberalizing trend.

Representative of Restif's method was his treatment of the swaddling of infants. Part of what the eighteenth century called *l'éducation physique*, swaddling was a popular topic among enlightened doctors. Four eminent medical men, Fourcroy de Guillerville, Desessartz, Deleurye, and Ballexserd, all adamantly advocated abandonment of the harmful and barbaric custom. Their arguments were reasonable enough. To wrap babies up in layer upon layer of cotton and wool, to pin the clothing and then to wrap a rope "four fingers thick" securely, from feet to shoulders, around the absurd costume, was more than overprotecting the child. Actual physical ailments resulted. "Blood and humors would build up on places less compressed, producing distensions and tumors that gradually hardened and disfigured the child." [25] But Restif, who tended to pick charlatans like Guilbert de Préval for his medical advisers, paid no heed to the reputable practitioners and disregarded this small advance in knowledge. The doctors only paid attention to the physical effects of swaddling; Restif was interested in a broader issue.

[25] Jean Charles Desessartz, *Traité de l'éducation corporelle des enfans en bas âge, ou Reflexions pratiques sur les moyens de procurer une meillure constitution aux citoyens* (Paris: Herissant, 1760), p. 93.

For him, the important result of swaddling was psychological; a baby wrapped up tightly from birth would have a weak will and would always feel repressed and submissive. In utopia, the arrangement logically followed Restif's intuitions.

Girls being throughout life in a different position from men, must have an absolutely different education, beginning immediately after birth. Girls will be swaddled. . . . The movements of the girl must be curbed and restricted from the first instant of her life.[26]

Male babies, on the other hand, were afforded complete freedom of movement. Parents had to be particularly careful to provide loose-fitting garments and a sleeping area with plenty of room for a restless lad.[27] Thereby, Restif's ideal personality types would be reinforced. Females would grow up with a sense that they must control themselves to comply with some external force; males would mature with a feeling of effectiveness and power. A girl strapped up tightly as an infant would not contradict the wishes of her husband. This is the kind of technique Restif recommended for the restoration of order in human relationships through education.

At each stage of the educative process, Restif sought the best means of imprinting his models into the character of children. The project, as he saw it, demanded repressive laws that would force children into society's mold. An idealized image of Lycurgus was Restif's authority. Like the Lacedaemonian, he felt that severe restriction was the method appropriate to the task of civilizing children. The basic precepts of education were set forth as absolutes and the slightest misdemeanor would incur heavy penalties. Utopia would not tolerate an idle, carefree childhood. Boys and girls would learn early and learn well the limits society set upon their freedom. At no time was life soft for the masculine sex, as they were being trained for dominance and willfulness. Directly from Charles Rollin's description of ancient Sparta came Restif's command that boys would be exposed to extreme "heat and cold, hunger and thirst" in order to make them tough.[28] To become masculine, boys must be prevented from day-dreaming about girls, by making ". . . them so busy that the passions are forced into silence until the age of twenty-one."[29]

Girls received an opposite but equally determined education. To make

[26] *Les Gynographes*, p. 63.
[27] *L'Andrographe*, p. 32.
[28] *Ibid.*, p. 36.
[29] *Ibid.*, p. 14.

their wills pliable, Restif did not separate girls by age group. Living together, the younger girls would learn to bend to the whims of their elders.[30] Naturally girls needed no intellectual training; even the elementary skills of reading and writing were unnecessary for women.[31] Going against the trend begun near the end of the seventeenth century by Fénelon's *De l'éducation des filles* and continued in the eighteenth century by many enlightened writers like Madame d'Epinay,[32] Restif denied the need to instruct women in the higher arts. This would only divert them from their primary task of pleasing their husbands. Although enlightened theorists had become impatient with traditional methods that kept women in darkness and proposed to include women in the future society by instructing them, Restif returned to an older view.

A deep contradiction in Restif's educational thought emerges from our analysis of his method of instruction. At one level, he claimed that sexual identity was nature's law, which implied that if children were left to nature sexual identity would easily be achieved. Yet the utopian training was anything but permissive. The most harsh impositions were placed on youth. Utopian education was to be at once natural and artificial. The only conclusion possible is that Restif never resolved this conflict in his thought. To make matters even more complicated, he was not even consistent in calling for a repressive education. In Megapatagonia, the chief utopia in *La Découverte australe par un homme volant* (1781), an entirely opposite tone was given to education. The Megapatagon children needed no discipline at all to form perfect characters; they were considered moral at birth.

. . . youth has a just spirit. It feels strongly that [society's] precepts are reasonable, and it conforms scrupulously in its conduct. This is the source of the harmony that . . . reigns among us. All young people work, occupy themselves, lead an active, useful life without any commandments.[33]

On the issue of repression or laxity in teaching, Restif presented two diametrically opposed views. He asserted that the education of sexual identity called for either no laws at all or a barrage of austere regulations.

E. EIGHTEENTH-CENTURY THEORIES OF EDUCATION

Theories of education abounded in eighteenth-century France. Most philosophers, moralists, and utopians found a place in their thoughts for

---

[30] *Les Gynographes*, p. 64.
[31] *L'Andrographe*, p. 10.
[32] *Lettres à mon fils* (Paris: Sauton, 1869).
[33] *La Découverte australe*, III, 485.

the training and instruction of youth. There were two obvious reasons for this. First, the Jesuits, the traditional schoolmasters of France, were in conflict with the new secular thought. A system of education was required which would replace the constrictions of theology. Second, Lockean epistemology, as interpreted by Condillac and Helvétius in France, gave a large role to education in the cultivation of human rationality. Sensationalist theories of knowledge, banishing the concept of innate ideas, defined man as a product of his environment. Climate, custom, and education determined much of man's behavior. The task of education was nothing less than transforming a natural, primitive child into a benevolent, social adult. The important issues remained: what was to be educated in man and how repressive should education be?

The best answers to the latter question had been given by Rousseau and Helvétius before Restif wrote. To what extent did morality derive from nature and to what extent from society? Hence, how great a role should be given to the educator in the child's development? Helvétius [34] presented the case for the complete formation of man's being by society: for him, the moral was synonymous with the social. Rousseau's *Emile* advocated the opposite position: the more education fostered the natural, the more moral the adult would be. As we have seen, Restif's utopia called for both methods without any reconciliation of the differences between them.

The other question, what part of man should be educated, was answered by emphasizing either the rational faculty or the passions. Almost all theorists intended the education of the child as a whole, but inevitably stressed one or another of man's capacities at the expense of the others, depending on the assumptions of the theorists. The dominant tendency was to make education a matter of the instruction of the rational capacity of both boys and girls. Even those thinkers who included sexual identity in the sphere of education generally prescribed the cultivation of reason as the solution to all difficulties. In the utopias of Foigny [35] (1676) and Mercier (1770) the development of sexual identity was viewed as part of the intellectual improvement of mankind. Mercier, in *L'An 2440*, foresaw the consequences of masculine intellectual domination. "Women, instead of exercising their vanity, have cultivated their minds. . . ." [36]

[34] *De l'Homme* (London: n.p., 1786), II, p. 382.
[35] G. Foigny, *Les Avantures de Jacques Sadeur dans la découverte et le voiage de la Terre Australe* (Paris: Barbin, 1692), pp. 223–225.
[36] Trans. by W. Hooper as *Memoirs of the Year Two Thousand Five Hundred* (London: Robinson, 1772), II, 154.

A moralist who was representative of the thought on the education of sexual identity was Boudier de Villemert. First written in 1774 and later translated into English as *The Ladies' Friend, Being a Treatise on the Virtues and Qualifications Which Are the Brightest Ornaments of the Fair Sex and Render Them Most Agreeable to the Sensible Part of Mankind*,[37] Boudier's statement was an expression of a large section of educated opinion. It was popular enough to go through at least four editions in the English version. Boudier's theme, that vice resulted from the blurring of sexual lines, was tersely put:

The ladies (and the fault is ours) being thrown into a continual dissipation, for which they are not made, have contracted an inclination for what is frivolous, and even brought it into vogue. They have so far subjected the men to their caprices, that all distinction of the superiority of reason is lost; softness having . . . effeminated everything. The contrast, put by nature between the two sexes, is no longer to be seen. . . .[38]

Boudier's sentiment in this passage was typical though a trifle old-fashioned for the third quarter of the eighteenth century, mourning a lost simplicity of manners. To straighten out the chaotic moral circumstances, Boudier, conquering his penchant for the virtues of the ignorant woman of the past,[39] proposed opening the doors of wisdom and learning to the female sex, if only halfway. No heavy, abstruse matters for them—just some light science and history to stimulate their minds without bringing furrows to their pretty brows.[40]

The reason for bringing Boudier into the discussion is to emphasize the contrast between the general sensibility toward the sexes and Restif's. Restif focused on the moral problem described by Boudier; utopian education was not, however, designed for the advancement of reason in women. According to Restif, the good society encouraged and sustained the maximum difference between the personalities of the two sexes. Restif confronted the moral issue from a fresh perspective. For him, there were basic archetypes in the biological and psychic makeup of the two sexes. When they did not find channels for expression in society, the harmonious relations of the sexes were disrupted. In these cases man and wife could not get along with one another and satisfaction, sexual and otherwise, was sought outside the family. Adultery, jealousy, misunderstanding, hate, inebriation—the results were hyperbolic.

[37] (Philadelphia: M. Carey, 1793).
[38] *Ibid.*, p. 9.
[39] *Ibid.*, p. 17.
[40] *Ibid.*, p. 14.

Seething animosity in the home and debauchery outside destroyed the fabric of the family and with it, the education of the children. So the failure to achieve personal satisfaction in the relationship of man and wife influenced the whole moral tone of society: to this extent civilization actually disrupted the organization of the passions. Boudier's frivolous women and effeminate men had counterparts in everyday Parisian life. For Restif the well-being of France in the relatively untroubled eighteenth century led to "dissipation" and by the middle of the century manners were in need of purifying.

Never has the education of women been as poor as it is today, thanks to the rubbish of our philosophists, who preach only what is necessary for men. But when it is no longer a question of men, what will happen to us? I shake with indignation on seeing one woman adorned in a man's clothes. What will become of morals and knowledge? A female savant, a female reasoner are the most insupportable of women. Here is the advice that I give to men, waiting for education to become rational and in conformity with the aim of nature: if your Equals do not match you, and if their mothers have made them demanding, capricious, priggish, coquettes, lazy, heady, peevish, flighty . . . or if they are given faults equal to all these together and are made into prudes, disdain them, for God's sake! Come off your high horse and take women to whom you can say, without revolting them: "I want it; I need it." [41]

Eighteenth-century civilization defeated nature. Study in the arts and sciences, even the mere ability to read and write, had created pretentious women who could not respond to the call of love, who could not please.

Restif's notion of education was not a paideia in Werner Jaeger's sense; it was not an enriching ideal wherein the ego grew ever deeper, becoming ever more aware and self-consciously more powerful. On the contrary, Restif's way of molding natural man into a properly civilized form was to touch the lower depths of the soul. It was man's natural propensities that he sought to shape by utopian education. To him the real problem was that of socializing the passions.

. . . to have a good education, the passions must be regulated, moderated, held in a proper equilibrium. The flux and reflux of the passions is as necessary for the soul as the circulation of the blood and the humors is to the body . . . to seek to destroy them would be to go against the Supreme Being; it would be to attempt the impossible.[42]

What he meant by the passions and how he revalued them are topics discussed in the next chapter.

[41] *Le Nouvel Abeilard,* III, 373–374 *n.*
[42] *Le Paysan perverti,* II, 90.

Restif's conception of education was at odds with the general attitude of the Enlightenment. For the philosophes education was intimately connected with the progress of civilization. Education was, for them, the cultural vehicle of the perfection of humanity. Writing in one of his lighter esays, Kant argued the position of the Enlightenment: "It may be that education will constantly be improved, and that each succeeding generation will advance one step towards the perfecting of mankind; for with education is involved the great secret of the perfection of human nature." [43] While Kant's bright hopes for the future of man were expressed in moderate tones, Condorcet would later follow similar lines of thought—only with more force and conviction. Kant and Condorcet married education with a historical vision of man's progress; just this was entirely lacking in Restif's thought and consequently he placed much less emphasis on the instructional aspect of education. Reason, called judgment by Kant and science by Condorcet, was the secret to man's progress. Since Restif held no such notion of progress he had less need to educate the rational faculty.

Furthermore, the Enlightenment stressed reason and equality in education as prime foundation stones for building the Heavenly City on earth. Condorcet rejected the outmoded limitations on women: "I do not believe that there is any difference between women and men except what is the work of education. . . . the kind of constraints in which opinions relative to morals hold the soul and the mind of women from infancy . . . must destroy their progress in almost all areas." [44] The penchant of the eighteenth century for viewing all people as identical, interchangeable atoms in the social universe,[45] for prescribing all differences to the conditioning of the environment and invalidating them as unnatural, logically led to a demand for the equal education of boys and girls. If women are not physically men's equals, argued Condorcet, it does not follow that they are mentally inferior. One need only mention a few French women of letters to prove the point: Madame de La Fayette, Madame de Genlis, Madame de Sévigné.[46] To Restif, who looked not to the advance of consciousness but to order within the passions, Condorcet and the Enlightenment had gone astray. "Why do the pretended Philosophists today have the perfidy of wanting to lead the

---

[43] Emmanuel Kant, *Education* (Ann Arbor: University of Michigan, 1966), p. 7.

[44] Nicolas Caritat, Marquis de Condorcet, "Lettres d'un bourgeois de New Haven à un citoyen de Virginie," *Oeuvres* (Paris: Didot, 1847), IX, 18.

[45] Frank Manuel, "From Equality to Organicism," *Journal of the History of Ideas* January, 1956, pp. 17, 54, 69.

[46] Condorcet, *op. cit.*, IX, p. 19.

timid sex astray . . . ?" [47] The cry for equality was only a ruse, hiding the intention to make women just like men and sacrificing the wonders of difference.

Surely, our little philosophists, who make the two sexes equal, are correct, but not in the sense they think! They want women to be men. . . . Women have always had, for me, an inexpressible, ineffable charm. . . .[48]

Restif's answer to the "philosophists" was the education of sexual identity by implanting his models of masculinity and femininity in the children of utopia.

F. RESTIF AND ROUSSEAU

Restif's intellectual position in his age is better fixed in relation to a man who in some ways challenged the philosophes long before Condorcet wrote, namely, Rousseau. Restif has frequently been dismissed with the sobriquet *"le Rousseau du ruisseau."* [49] The intellectual paternity of Rousseau cannot be denied; to see the son as the mere tinsel copy of the father is an error.

Rousseau is the name most frequently found in Restif's utopian writings, many times simply with the familiar "J.-J." In fact the epigraph on the title page of *L'Andrographe* is from Rousseau. The titles, no less than the conceptions, of some of Restif's books derive from him: *Le Nouvel Abeilard* for *La Nouvelle Héloïse, Le Nouvel Emile* for *Emile, Monsieur Nicolas* for *Les Confessions. Le Nouvel Emile* was intended as a "supplement" to *Emile.* [50] In *Monsieur Nicolas*, Restif applauded Rousseau and himself as the only two men who "had clear ideas about education." [51] According to biographers, they never met and never wrote to one another. That Rousseau knew of Restif is proven by a letter written by the former to Costard, a publisher, and printed in *Monsieur Nicolas.* [52] In the letter Rousseau praises Restif for *Le Nouvel Emile.* The authenticity of the letter has been accepted by scholars, though there are grounds for doubt since Rousseau writes precisely what Restif would have liked to hear.

[47] *Les Gynographes*, p. 203.
[48] *Lettres inédites de Restif de Labretone* (Nantes: Forest and Grimaud, 1883), p. 21.
[49] Marc Chadourne, *Restif de la Bretonne, ou le Siècle prophétique* (Paris: Hachette, 1958), VI, p. vii.
[50] *Monsieur Nicolas*, Pauvert edition, VI, 558.
[51] *Ibid.*, VI, 60.
[52] *Ibid.*, VI, 48.

In thought and expression Rousseau and Restif turned away from the abstract rationalism and sensationalism of the philosophes. Both were pre-Romantics, glorifying sensibility and attacking the presumptions of cosmopolitan, civilized society. Both extolled the primitive, were fascinated by it, but ultimately rejected it as an ideal for France. Unlike the philosophes, both formulated separate theories of education for women. The last chapter of *Emile* is devoted to instructing Sophie. While the philosophes pondered the school curriculum and sought to substitute scientific subjects for religious, practical for theoretical, modern languages for Greek and Latin, Rousseau and Restif emphasized the necessity of education outside and before formal schooling.

Their originality lay in seeing the child as a unique person and his needs as peculiar to his state in life. Even Locke still treated the child largely as a diminutive adult, with the result that to him education meant the development and exercise of the rational faculty. Here, in *Emile*, is an unparalleled glorification of childhood.

Childhood has its own ways of seeing, thinking, and feeling; nothing is more foolish than to try and substitute our ways. . . .[53]

When I think of a child of ten or twelve, strong, healthy, well-grown for his age, only pleasant thoughts are called up, whether of the present or the future. I see him keen, eager, and full of life, free from gnawing cares and painful forebodings, absorbed in this present state, and delighting in a fullness of life which seems to extend beyond himself. . . . I watch the child with delight, I picture to myself the man with even greater pleasure.[54]

If Rousseau saw childhood as man's springtime, deserving the enjoyment of its own pleasures and uncramped by Latin textbooks, Restif concurred and added the dimension of dawning sexuality to innocent youth. Recalling his own experiences, he claimed that children retain memories of being fondled in the erogenous zones and of seeing adults in the sex act.

[At the age of four] I used . . . to be fondled—and very ardently!—by Marie, and carried in her arms to Vespers. I am forced to describe her caresses, since they have been prejudicial not to my morals only, but to my health; for the memory of them overstimulated my fiery imagination before I had come to my full strength. Marie used to kiss me on the cheek, and upon my lips . . . she went further, though in all innocence on her part; she put her hand under my little petticoats and amused herself by gently slapping and tickling me. She went further yet . . . and then she would devour me with kisses. . . .[55]

[53] Jean Jacques Rousseau, *Emile*, trans. by B. Foxley (London: Dent, 1963), p. 54.
[54] *Ibid.*, pp. 122–123.
[55] *Monsieur Nicolas*, Ellis edition, I, 86.

He tells of another unforgettable experience when he accidentally came upon a married couple making love: "[This] proves how dangerous it is for a husband and wife to behave freely in the presence of children, even when these innocents are not of an age to understand." [56]

Such perceptions were not noted by Rousseau in *Emile*. To Restif, at the mercy of his own highly passionate nature, these thoughts were of primary significance for the utopian educator. Often he returned to the theme of the necessity of minimizing the child's sensual experience. [57]

The central question for the theory of education and the point where Restif both agrees and disagrees with Rousseau is repression: put in eighteenth-century terms, shall children be educated according to nature or according to society? In this respect, *Emile* can be viewed as a continuation of the trends of the two *Discours;* the education of the child is designed to enable him to withstand the approbation elicited by civil society. Rousseau's argument is, by 1762, more fully developed and more shaded, but the program of the *Encyclopédie*, the advancement of the arts and sciences, with its urbane, cosmopolitan implications, is still the object of his scorn. A tense, parallel cadence announces his thunder:

Our wisdom is slavish prejudice, our customs consist in control, constraint, compulsion. Civilized man is born and dies a slave. The infant is bound up in swaddling clothes, the corpse is nailed down in his coffin. All his life long man is imprisoned by our institutions. [58]

Civilization creates desires in man which are painful and cannot be satisfied. [59] To avoid this, the child must be secluded from other people. "Keep the child dependent on things only. By this course of education you will have followed the order of nature." [60]

Rousseau demands a permissive education, the child to be left to nature. "Emile, who has been brought up in full freedom like young peasants and savages, should behave like them and change as he grows up." [61] Restif not only agrees with Rousseau but claims priority. "J.-J. R. recognized that fine truth, the foundation of his *Emile:* that man must seem to have been reared by Nature. And, though younger, I recognized it before him, very strongly. . . ." [62] Restif's claim is almost empty of

[56] *Ibid.*, I, 87.
[57] *Les Gynographes*, pp. 11, 25, 35–36, 63; and *L'Andrographe*, pp. 37, 41, 156.
[58] Rousseau, *op. cit.*, p. 10.
[59] *Ibid.*, p. 44.
[60] *Ibid.*, p. 49.
[61] *Ibid.*, p. 280.
[62] *Les Nuits de Paris*, 11, 2513–2514.

meaning since "nature" is not defined. Also, Restif did not grasp the complexity of Rousseau's thought. To him, Rousseau was the progenitor of a permissive education that instructed the child only to be "ignorant." [63] He failed to notice that Rousseau also saw to the social needs of Emile. Interestingly enough, Restif recognized only the side of Rousseau that inveighed against civilization and glorified the natural propensities of the individual. The Rousseau of the *Contrat social*, who opted for the submission of the individual to the general will, he overlooked. Consequently, Restif found himself at odds with his master and returned to the necessity of shaping the passions for social use. "Although it be proven that solitary education would be the most advantageous for the conservation of innocence; nonetheless, as men are made to live in society, it will be more useful to sacrifice something of man's inherent goodness to the advantage of sociability. . . ." [64]

Restif discovered that Paris had taken to *Emile*, though the results were not uniformly happy. Parisians had heeded Rousseau and nursed their babies by themselves, ending the practice of hiring wet nurses. Restif believed the effects were disastrous because the milk of these "civilized" mothers was not healthy or nourishing.[65] The new method disturbed the emotional development of the children and led to a loss of order and discipline in the household. Restif's real or imagined fears aside, his ideal educator, while claiming to follow nature's dictates, would take an active part in the child's life and would be more repressive than Rousseau's ideal tutor.

For Rousseau, nature was moral; it was good and any tampering with it by man resulted in corruption and artificiality. Still, in Sophie's training Rousseau called for a strict submission to her husband's wishes: ". . . habitual restraint produces a docility which woman requires . . . she should early learn to submit to injustice and to suffer the wrongs inflicted on her by her husband without complaint. . . ." [66] Rousseau's turnabout here is without explanation. Sophie's education is only justified by Emile and does not imply the valuation of women so much a part of Restif's utopia. Rousseau restricted the place of women to mere instruments for the pleasure of men, whereas Restif made a deliberate effort to structure society around the specific needs of women as he saw them.

[63] *Les Gynographes*, p. 203.
[64] *L'Andrographe*, p. 39.
[65] *Les Nuits de Paris*, pp. 11, 2513–2514.
[66] Rousseau, *op. cit.*, p. 333.

III

Love

A. LOVE AND THE UTOPIANS

From the Renaissance, the Morean model of the contemplative ideal of life had dominated the French concept of the good society. In a utopian novel published in 1676 Gabriel Foigny, a monk of unconventional stamp, exemplified the extent to which love was taken as an inferior, if not a tainted, human emotion. So repulsed was he by the passions that he envisioned man in his utopian society in Australia as an hermaphrodite, thus dismissing both the need and the capacity for sensual love. Because he reproduced by himself, Foigny's utopian had developed his rational faculty to control his passions. Love in Australia was "neither carnal nor brutal"; it lacked "the ardor of animals." [1] Australians felt toward one another only a "cordial love" which they gave to all their fellow utopians equally.[2] In Foigny's ideal society sensual love was replaced by a weaker feeling, politeness.

On the other hand, the French utopians of the eighteenth century began to envisage erotic gratification as the central purpose in the ideal society. During this age of eudaemonism, happiness on the perfect island was characterized by the carefree enjoyment of the delights of love. Travels of discovery to exotic, primitive lands were important in the sensate utopias. After Cook and Bougainville issued reports on their explorations in Tahiti, Diderot capitalized on the general interest they evoked from Europeans by using Polynesia as the basis of his attacks on

[1] G. Foigny, *Les Avantures de Jacques Sadeur dans la découverte et le voiage de la Terre Australe* (Paris: Barbin, 1692) p. 132.

[2] Negly and Patrick, *The Quest for Utopia* (New York: Anchor Books, 1962), p. 397.

33

the outmoded asceticism of the Old World. In *Supplément au voyage de Bougainville* (1772), he set an idyll of pure love against the complex repressions of civilization. What was a crime in Europe was innocent pleasure in Tahiti. To Diderot love was gentle; tender caresses and soft flutes signaled a calm utopia of love.

. . . the young Tahitian girl yielded herself to the transports and embraces of the Tahitian youth. . . . She was proud to excite the desire and to attract the amorous glances of unknown men, of relatives, of her brother. Without dread and without shame, in our presence, in the midst of a circle of innocent Tahitians, to the sound of flutes, between the dances, she accepted the caresses of the one to whom her young heart and the secret voice of her senses urged her.[3]

As the utopians investigated love anew, the emotion became shaded by the pastel sensibility of rococo France. Love was dreamed of as a gentle melody toned by pastoral pipes. On Morelly's "Floating Islands" (1753), eros was a tender, uninhibited joy, distant from the cramping controls of civilization.

Closer to the end of the century, Restif and Sade retained the concept of eros as the cornerstone of the ideal city, but drastically altered the tone. Diderot and Morelly had dreamed of a soft, vernal love that could rejuvenate a tired civilization; Restif and Sade stressed the violence and cruelty of the passions—a destructiveness that threatened the very possibility of morality.

B. Restif's Rules for Love

1. Free Love

The purpose of Restif's utopia was to create an ideal environment for the gratification of the passions. In the imaginary-voyage novel *La Découverte australe par un homme volant* (1781), Restif stretched his creative powers to devise social institutions suited to amorous felicity. In this orderly ideal society, certain innovations designed to permit a full gratification of sensuality in marriage could eventually be made without danger. Girls were to receive sexual instruction to better enable them to please their husbands and enjoy love themselves.[4]

I would like to see "initiations" established such as were practiced by the ancients. . . . Female initiations or mysteries were entirely different from those of the male. . . . [Elder women] taught girls the pretty ways to capti-

[3] Denis Diderot, *Interpreter of Nature*, trans. by J. Steward and J. Kemp (New York: International Publishers Co., 1963), pp. 156–157.

[4] *L'Andrographe*, p. 163.

vate a man . . . : the voluptuous grace, of a deportment that excites desire. They went further and expounded the whole art of venery: of lascivious kisses and amorous handling. . . . Nowadays the happiness of the human race is left to chance. Only prostitutes make a study of this art. . . .[5]

Enlightenment replaced anxiety and ignorance of the facts of life. In one utopia in Australia a completely permissive attitude was envisaged. Divorce was permitted at will and the couple had only to wait one year to remarry.[6] Marriage itself was only temporary, lasting for one year. The advantages were plain: adultery, seduction, and rape were unknown in this community.[7] The general effects on the utopians were more remarkable. "The entire nation seemed renewed: old age has disappeared in the two sexes; everyone dressed up, everyone friendly, everyone gay and healthy, they aspired equally after the pleasures that a new choice would promise them. . . ."[8] Freedom in love opened new vistas for human vitality and the atmosphere of the utopian plan foretold unknown improvement for the human race.

Perhaps Restif's most practical reform related to love was his humane approach to prostitution. Public conscience was not greatly aroused by this social problem in the eighteenth century. That statistics are hard to find and unreliable is an acid test of indifference. One source claimed that in 1784, 60,000 public and 10,000 private prostitutes worked in Paris, earning an estimated 143,800,000 livres.[9] Considering that the total population of Paris was less than one million, the figures seem highly exaggerated. A plan for state control of prostitutes was drawn up by the jurist Aulas but never carried out. Another attempt to regulate them, this time by the police commission in 1763, also failed. Even Mercier, who pondered the reform of many social evils, merely condemned and outlawed prostitutes in his utopia.[10]

Le Pornographe, ou Idées d'un honnête homme sur un projet de règlement pour les prostituées was the earliest volume of the Idées singulières. Restif began writing the book while on a trip from Paris to his home in Sacy. He had been unable to formulate his ideas on this unsavory subject in the sanctified atmosphere of his youth. When completed the book was a product of personal experience, not the reflections of a

[5] Monsieur Nicolas, Ellis edition, V, 337–338.

[6] La Découverte australe, III, 489.

[7] Ibid., III, 501–502.

[8] Ibid., III, 526.

[9] Iwan Bloch, Rétif de la Bretonne (Berlin: Harrwitz, 1906), p. 504.

[10] Sébastien Mercer, L'An 2440, trans. by W. Hooper as Memoirs of The Year Two Thousand Five Hundred (London: Robinson, 1772), I, 205.

saintly philantropist. I take exception here with Tabarant's unsubstantiated assertion that Restif knew nothing of Parisian brothels and that *Le Pornographe* "is completely foreign to the realities of prostitution of the time, and the world in which he leads us can only be called Utopia." The scholar does not seem to realize that the reforms planned in *Le Pornographe* were precisely utopian. Tabarant weakly answers Restif's claim that "I have visited public women in 1755, 6, 7, 8, 9; in 1761, 2, 3, 4, 5, 6, 7, 8, 9, in order to write *Le Pornographe*," with an estimate that Restif could not afford the fare.[11] Restif's erotic needs drove him to the public houses where he allegedly met other notorious luminaries, among them Sade. Restif knew well the histories and misfortunes of prostitutes. He rescued one, Zéphire, from her fate and almost married her. Her story has the pathos of the innocent girl put in a brothel by her mother because of poverty.

The model for *Le Pornographe* was, again, Restif's image of Sparta.[12] Following the ancients, his purpose was to transform prostitutes from downtrodden, diseased women on the fringes of society, into members of a respected profession with a useful social function to perform.[13] He maintained that there was nothing intrinsically evil in prostitution; the fault lay in society's treatment of it. Prostitutes were looked upon as objects; they were "automatized."[14] Although degraded by fate and poverty,[15] they were human beings and deserved respect. After the reform they would be able to enjoy their work with dignity, no longer slaves to the execrable caprices of libertines.[16] In Paris, with its blunted sensibility, the prostitutes had to submit to cruelty in order to provide stimuli intense enough to give satisfaction to their customers. The reform was directed, typically, at renewing the prostitutes' capacity to please by a comprehensive refashioning of all aspects of their trade.

Le Pornographe was based on the assumption that sensual love is a human capacity that cannot be dismissed by theological or moral arguments. In defense of his ideas, Restif stretched the theory of social utilitarianism to cover prostitution: rapes and seductions would be banished,[17] the children of prostitutes would be properly cared for,[18] the population

[11] Adolphe Tabarant, *Le Vrai visage de Restif de la Bretonne* (Paris: Editions Montaigne, 1936), pp. 152–153.
[12] *Le Pornographe*, pp. 19, 163–164.
[13] *Ibid.*
[14] *Ibid.*, p. 169.
[15] *Ibid.*, p. 171.
[16] *Ibid.*, p. 164.
[17] *Ibid.*, p. 34.
[18] *Ibid.*, p. 35.

would be increased (considered an absolute good until the time of Malthus). So pleased was he with his project that, without foundation in fact, he fantasized its adoption by Joseph II.[19] Restif's source was the announcement in *Gazette de Leyde*, at the end of 1786, of Joseph II's liberal reform of the civil code. The conclusions Restif drew from the permissive tone of the code indicate perhaps a touch of egocentrism more than the popularity of *Le Pornographe*. There are indications, however, that Joseph did at least read *Le Pornographe* and think highly enough of it to express his gratitude to Restif by sending him a portrait embossed with diamonds and a diploma dubbing Restif a baron. Proof of the honor comes from a letter written by Restif's grandson after Restif's death.[20] But even the revolutionary Joseph II was not radical enough to legalize prostitution. His reform of the criminal code of 1786, which according to Restif legalizes the proposals of *Le Pornographe*, imposed severe punishments on prostitutes and did not take up Restif's suggestions.[21] In reality, few people would tolerate such a frank treatment of sensual love; few could forget the sordid and base qualities of prostitution long enough to look at it with clear eyes.[22]

In the later volumes of the *Idées singulières* dealing wtih utopian institutions, prostitution was not considered—not because it was evil but because it would have no social utility; the causes for its existence in Paris would be eliminated. Inequality, luxury, above all, a loss of sexual identity—these social vices created the need for the legitimate but less than ideal gratifications of the brothel. Thus at the public houses of Paris ". . . men are found in great numbers as wealth becomes more unequal, and as a necessary consequence, morals are weak, effeminate, disordered in [men]; low, servile, easy to corrupt in [women]." [23] Civilized life in Paris corrupted the passions and set them loose as monsters, breathing cruelty and perversion from their unnatural mouths. Love had become not the free, innocent pleasure that nature intended, but a violent, insatiable ogre.

2. Toward a Religion of Love

There was another dimension to Restif's idea of love that is felt but not prominent in the code for marriage. More was at stake than social

---

[19] *Monsier Nicolas*, Ellis edition, V, 395, and *Le Palais Royal*, p. 145.

[20] See J. Rives Childs, *Restif de la Bretonne* (Paris: Briffaut, 1949), p. 57.

[21] See *The Emperor's New Code of Criminal Laws* (Dublin: Rea, 1787), p. 108.

[22] For the opinions of contemporaries on *Le Pornographe*, see Childs, *op. cit.*, pp. 15, 16, 18, 28, 39.

[23] *Le Pornographe*, pp. 5–6.

harmony in these regulations. Restif struggled with a new metaphysic: love was elevated to an absolute value. A world of sensate pleasure, utopia also needed an ultimate justification of the ways of nature. Restif felt impelled to elaborate a quasi-religion for his ideal society, with love as its foundation. When he asserted, "Love and life are the same thing. . . ." [24] he overstepped the boundaries of social reform. His claim for the absolute worth of love placed him at the beginning of a train of thought that attempted to fill the spiritual vacuum left by an impotent Christianity. The next generation of utopians, notably Fourier, Saint-Simon, the Saint-Simonians, and Comte, were to invent extravagant forms of a religion of love. As a precursor of this group, Restif's metaphysic of love proves interesting.

When Restif peered into the starry heavens he did not see a great Chain of Being, nor did he hear the music of the spheres or even the ticking of the Deists' clock; he witnessed the "copulation" of the sun and the planets. All matter was alive and emitting or receiving seminal fluid; the sun gave forth light which fertilized the planets. Nature consisted only of living matter, and this was divided into the male and the female. The *telos* of nature was inherent in its structure; to reproduce, to love, was the purpose of all life. The whole universe copulated and derived its deepest happiness from this act. "The act of generation is the primary pleasure for all beings." [25] Just as Restif's cosmogony was colored by a primitive anthropomorphism, so his notion of love reflected a mind in contact with the primeval forces of life. Love was the ancient natural law that provided the framework for human action. As the ultimate basis of life, love was an instinctual necessity, negating choice and freedom. This law of nature was not to be unveiled by reason, but was involuntary, like hunger.[26] A utopian society based on love was therefore in conformity with the necessity of nature. Participation in the practices prescribed by the social regulations of love was not only legal and moral; it provided the actual *feeling* of existence. Thus the act of loving one's wife put one in harmony with nature; individual existence and universal destiny were bound together; certainty and meaning deepened the experience of biological need. Love became a ritual act.

Restif, incidentally, joined in most of the occult movements of his day—Eastern religions, mesmerism, and other novelties—which were more

---

[24] *Les Gynographes,* p. 250.
[25] *Monsieur Nicolas,* Pauvert edition, V, 268.
[26] *Le Nouvel Emile,* II, 266–267.

popular than is generally believed. Auguste Viatte [27] suggests that Restif's cosmogony was influenced by Bonneville. If this was the case, Boneville's ideas must have been communicated orally, because the only book by Bonneville I have been able to locate was written well after *La Découverte australe* (1781), which contained Restif's first statement of his cosmogony.

Restif was not alone in insisting that physical laws and moral laws were identical; [28] in the eighteenth century the attempt to equate the two orders was widespread. [29] Usually, impetus for making the identification came from the desire to find a moral equivalent for Newton's all-embracing physical law of gravity. Restif's solution was unique. Happiness was the greatest good for utopians and it resulted only from pleasurable sensations which, in turn, were produced by the act of love or by the release of passion. There was a God in Restif's universe who resembled the Deist's God in that he was the remote force which gave momentum to all matter. But in Restif's strange vision this God was composed of pure passion; God was pure "intellectual, electric, magnetic light"; he was seminal fluid. Restif believed that life was propagated by the emission of this substance which contained seeds and was transmitted from the male to the female who fertilized the seeds by providing a nesting place for them, during the act of love. The physical law that explained life was hence equated with the moral law of happiness.

In *La Découverte australe par un homme volant* and in *Monsieur Nicolas* Restif summarized all known explanations of the nature of the universe from the mythology of the ancients to the experimental science of Laplace. His object was to show the superiority of his own vitalist cosmology. His weird system was pantheistic, since God as pure vital fluid was present in all things; materialistic, for no nonmaterial substance existed; evolutionary, as the form of beings was always in transformation; irrational, since reason had very little to do with the nature of man or with anything else; and above all, vitalist, for the whole universe was dependent on the mating of male and female beings who continued the life cycle. Pantheism, materialism, evolution, irrationalism, and vitalism—what a peculiar combination of doctrines for the eighteenth century!

[27] *Les Sources occultes du romantisme* (Paris: Champion, 1965), 2 vols. This is a good "textbook" on such pre-Romantic extravagances; see especially Volume I for illuminism and theosophy, and pages 251–261 for Viatte's treatment of Restif.

[28] For example see *Monsieur Nicolas*, Pauvert edition, VI, 33, 50.

[29] Lester Crocker, *Nature and Culture* (Baltimore: Johns Hopkins, 1963), p. 332; B. Willey, Eighteenth-Century Background (Boston: Beacon, 1962), 137.

This new religion of love marked a sharp turning away from dry, mechanistic rationalism and experimentalism toward the organicist and illuminist doctrines that flooded France in the last years of the century, epitomized by Mesmer. In the utopian tradition, Fourier especially was to propound a similar vision in the next generation.

Implicit in Restif's natural philosophy or religion of love was a threat of satiation. Restif's universe was finite. A fixed quantity of animated matter existed eternally and was in perpetual transformation. Man's passions and capacity to love were also limited. Restif had no Rabelaisian sense of overflowing energy, only the eternal flux and reflux of the passions. On the national level, he substituted a feeling of the scarcity of love for the finite amount of bullion in mercantilist theory.[30] To be sure, individual sensibility could affect the amplitude of the passions slightly—this was minor. Of more importance were social institutions. When they were not properly formed to keep the passions in relative harmony, both satiation and debauchery, a drying up and an overflowing, would result. In Paris, which Restif ranked as a poor social system, the passions flowed not from excited love to calm love but from violent orgies to utter indifference. He lambasted Sade as the paradigm of a Parisian.

3. Marriage

The glorification of sensual love and the elevation of the sexual act to the status of the sacred represented only one side of Restif's concept of love. A deeper look at the organization of love, especially in *L'Andrographe* and *Les Gynographes*, reveals the tightest and most severe regulation of the passions imaginable. The rules pertaining to the institution of marriage displayed the extent to which love was to be inhibited in utopia, manifesting a blueprint of the divided nature of Restif's dreams. At the bottom of his utopian vision was a polarity marking Restif's swing from an exaltation of sensate delights to a demand for their strict renunciation.

At their worst, marriages in France were business affairs conducted to suit the interest of the parents. Doweries and social position were the components of this unromantic calculus of love. Engagements were arranged as soon as prospective brides and grooms were born. Mismatches, endemic to such an economizing system of love, were adjusted by intricate networks of liaisons.

Marriages in utopia were to be arranged on the basis of a "moral register" which kept track of the virtues and vices of every utopian from

---

[30] *Monsieur Nicolas*, Pauvert edition, V, 286.

the first cry of life to the last moan of death. Upon attaining young adulthood, boys of twenty-one and girls of eighteen would be assembled in two rows facing each other—place in line determined one's balance in the moral register. The higher a boy ranked, the more beautiful (and the more ethical, since Restif identified the two) his bride would be. Restif banished "caprice" and "interest" from marriages [31] only to make matches the result of long years of moral striving. Eros was a reward for strength of character; merit was the standard for love.

As the channel for love in utopia, marriage was a most crucial institution. Restif did all he could to invest it with the dignity of a secular sacrament. All through the years of education, youth was to be aware that its fate in marriage depended on the state of its page in the moral register. Marriages were to be celebrated as a holiday four times a year, with pomp and full public participation.[32] There were songs and dances as the boys and girls lined up in rank to take their mates: "marriage is a saintly state, and the act of marriage [is] the most respectable and most sacred of nature's mysteries." [33] Festivities were in order because the fruits of marriage, love's delights, were the most important values of utopia. Love was the happiness of life; it was the reason for utopia and it provided the rewards that utopia conferred.

To account for the inevitable difficulties of the utopian institutions in satisfying everyone's needs in love, Restif wrote a play called *L'An deux mille* (1789). In it he contemplated the circumstance of two men in love with the same woman. In the play, Hardion and Unitanville both love Desiree, but Hardion is second in rank and has to relinquish his choice to Unitanville, the first. Since happiness can be found only in love and his whole fate is at stake, Hardion decides to rebel against the law of utopia. "What does it matter," he moans, "if the law makes me unhappy?" [34] Justice conflicts with happiness. The dilemma is important for, in the context of utopia, the gratification of love is the very purpose of society. Hardion says that he wants "to destroy this severe government. I am in despair! . . . Oh, if I could only live in happy times when all passions would have a free course!" [35] To deny Hardion's claim would mean that utopia falls short of perfection. Therefore the climax of the drama comes when Hardion, forced to resign himself to the loss of Desiree, accepts the mate that society provides. Utopian society cannot toler-

[31] *L'Andrographe*, p. 53 and *La Découverte australe*, III, 488–489.
[32] *L'Andrographe*, p. 54.
[33] *Ibid.*, p. 58.
[34] *Le Thesmographe*, p. 542.
[35] *Ibid.*, p. 548.

ate any deviation from its regulations. Love is the issue important enough to call utopian laws into question, but the sanctity of society's repressions cannot be broken.

It is interesting to note that other utopian writers wrestled with the same problem—the love of two men for the same woman—with no more satisfactory results. In *Supplément au voyage de Bougainville*, Diderot's Tahitians were not jealous enough to resent a second lover. In his earlier utopia, Berington permissively awarded the girl to one of the lovers after he threatened suicide.[36]

Although the assignment of mates could not satisfy everyone, Restif guaranteed that once married the utopians' enjoyment of love would be optimal. The danger for utopian couples was not so much incompatibility as boredom or satiation of desire. With this in mind, Restif designed utopian marital regulations to limit intercourse between the newlyweds. For fifteen years after marriage the couple lived apart, with their parents.[37] Officially, the girl's parents had to try to prevent sexual meetings, and the husband had to use his wits to obtain his bride for the night by circumventing the watch of the parents. His success was not punished, however, but received with public acclaim, and if his wife became pregnant his valor was praised even more.[38] Restif's intention was clear. Sensual pleasure was turned into a sport, enhancing its excitement. Also, as gratification was limited, it became more prized. With the danger of satiation averted, adultery became less frequent and order was returned to marital relations.

These marital laws were inspired by Plutarch's account of Sparta under Lycurgus.[39] The limits on the love-making of newlyweds in Sparta ". . . kept their bodies fruitful and the first ardor of their love fresh and unabated, for, as they were not satiated like those that are always with their wives, there still was room for unextinguished desire." [40] In the ancient Greek city there was a significant reason for the renunciation of love. Sparta was a military state and had to remain in constant readiness for war, and it was thought that the curb on sensuality helped keep the soldiers healthy. Restif had no such reason in mind. His regulations ap-

---

[36] Simon Berington, *The Adventures of Sig. G. di Lucca* (London: Pridden, 1776), p. 80.

[37] Vairesse's Sevarambians were also restricted for the first few years after marriage. See *Histoire des Sevarambes* in C. Garnier, *Voyages imaginaries* (Amsterdam: n.p., 1787–1789), V, 285.

[38] *L'Andrographe*, pp. 58–60.

[39] *Le Nouvel Abeilard*, III, 343, 344.

[40] *Plutarch's Lives*, trans. by J. and W. Langhorn (New York: Mentor, 1964), pp. 22–23.

pear all the more remarkable when we realize that he modeled his order of love on the military state of Lycurgus only to give love its full value. To prevent satiation and exacerbate the joys of love, restrictions were established in Megapatagonia. The sage Teugnil (the utopian form of Linguet) praised the mores of his countrymen to a less wise European visitor:

. . . since uncontrolled sensuality would cause great trouble, you may imagine that this is not the path we choose. We know that deprivations season pleasure and generate a hunger for it, so to speak. Therefore we have deprivations. There is, similarly, a form and a moderation in our pleasures. We never carry them to the point of utter satiety. But what strengthens good morals among us is that they are never left—as you have told me the case is in Europe —to individual caprice.[41]

Restif's reform of love in society consisted of meticulous restrictions with harsh sanctions for disobedience. The extent and severity of these controls were unequaled in the French utopian tradition.[42] Adultery, punished by prison, exile, or demotion to the lowest social rank, could easily be proved by the testimony of only one witness; mere suspicion of the crime was considered evidence of guilt. Women could obtain a divorce if their husbands beat them, drank heavily, or gambled in excess. Any familiarity between men and women was forbidden. Committees of women were established to "subject new brides to the most exact decency, forbidding all communication with men, sanctioned by the most severe penalties." [43] Yet this Draconian code was enacted for a society dedicated to love.[44] To cure Parisians of their frivolous attitude toward their mates, unrelenting strictness had to be enforced. Restif's own marriage to Agnès Lebégue was of the kind that needed this reform. A disastrous match punctuated by constant animosity, quarreling, bouts of violence, and adultery by both partners, it ended in separation. Utopia was an escape from these horrors into a calmer, more secure fantasy world, a world so antifeminist that "the most severe penalties" would be meted out to girls who "abandoned themselves to indecent bursts of laughter." [45]

[41] F. and F. Manuel, *French Utopias* (New York: Free Press, 1966), p. 173.

[42] See *L'Andrographe*, pp. 62–65, 95; *Les Gynographes*, pp. 78–79, 93–96, 104–105; *Le Thesmographe*, pp. 103–104; *Monsieur Nicolas*, Pauvert edition, VI, 66–69.

[43] *L'Andrographe*, p. 197.

[44] Morelly was also concerned with sexual relations in utopia, but his *Code de la nature* tended to be far more moderate: one year sufficed to purge adulterers of their sins. See Manuel and Manuel, *op. cit.*, p. 115.

[45] *Les Gynographes*, p. 96.

C. The Theory of the Passions

In its essential nature, passion exhibited to Restif two qualities characterized by "a flux and a reflux," imitating the ebb and flow motion that was at the heart of nature. There was only one undifferentiated substance called passion, but at a given moment passion could be either calm or violent. Appearing in Restif's pages as a primitive force or wave that engulfed the whole personality, this primal energy of life made man act in unexpected ways. The rational capacity, weak, frail, and hesitant, was undermined by the force of this natural power. What good were reason, benevolence, sociability, and morality when men felt moved by passion? [46]

Restif was not consistent in formally listing or classifying the passions. At one time, he divided them into three groups: pleasureful, painful, and mixed; at another, he listed over one hundred of them, using only the duality of agreeable and disagreeable, but giving each many subdivisions.[47] At bottom, however, only one passion was important to him: "the noblest, the one truly absorbing passion: love." [48]

A notorious incident in Restif's life illustrates his idea of the qualities of love. When he was sixteen years old his father sent him to work in the Fournier printing shop in Auxerre. He soon became enchanted by the owner's wife, a respectable woman ten years his senior. Her fictitious name, in *Monsieur Nicolas*, was Colette Parangon. Although she returned at least part of his emotion, Colette would not yield her honor. Frustrated beyond his negligible powers of continence, Restif forced his passions upon her, or at least made a violent attempt. His autobiography, an alleged "natural history" of the human heart and its passions, confessed and excused the deed on the grounds that the power of the passions is too strong to resist:

> this passion [became an] extreme obsession. . . . I protest that neither of us was to blame . . . or I alone. . . . But no, even I, the aggressor was not . . . I . . . man cannot be accounted guilty of that which is beyond his mortal strength, robbing him of reason and self-control. A dangerous principle, I know, but I am obliged to speak the truth; I know within myself that I was not to blame in anything which concerned my passion for Colette. I was not free; I was borne along against my will; I did everything I could to subdue myself and overcome my passion; to avoid my fall. . . . I seemed possessed by a fatality. . . .[49]

[46] *Les Gynographes*, p. 14.
[47] *Le Nouvel Emile*, II, 267; *Le Nouvel Abeilard*, III, 236–240.
[48] *Monsieur Nicolas*, Ellis edition, I, 63.
[49] *Ibid.*, II, 124.

Release from guilt by exposing it in writing was as necessary to Restif as it was obvious to his readers. Given this notion of man's passions, the difficulty of judging human conduct was great. If passion, the motive force of life, left man without free will, what room was there for moral choice? Was man a mere slave? Were not all ethical judments precluded and the "ought" dimension of experience invalidated? Restif's theory of the passions did in fact deny freedom of will to large segments of experience, but at the same time it was the springboard to utopia and to a new morality.

In utopia, the passions had to be regulated to preserve order. Once the passion of love was somewhat controlled—by the education of sexual identities for example—human interaction was possible, and thus a margin of freedom was established. Utopia was a system of constraints or limits and to the extent that the individual utopian adjusted to the social order, accepted its limits, he had freedom to enjoy love. A terrible force that overwhelmed man, love was nevertheless the deep joy of utopians.[50] Restif's utopia of the passions dug an awful gulf between the needs of eros and the demands of civilization, only to proclaim love as the purpose of that civilization.

The experience of love had to be heightened to dignify life with a purpose, yet the passions had to be strictly channeled to avoid anarchy and prevent the seduction of Madame Parangon. Hume had also set forth a morality based on emotion; the groundwork of moral acts was moral sentiments, among which benevolence stood highest. Restif's moral passions were quite different from the benevolence of the civilized man. The new dimension that had to be taken into account was the violence and destructiveness of the passions. Destructiveness could not be discarded for the sake of the gentleness of civilized sociability because it was a natural part of the passions; it was not a "monster" that was outside the harmony of nature but integral to that harmony.

To Restif, the social organization of the passions in contemporary France was woefully inadequate. Man's capacity for emotive expression was corrupted by the misplaced shackles of civilization. High among the causes of this condition Restif placed Christianity.

Our social order is detestable! I cannot conceive what puritanical and destructive genius has possessed the human race since the Christian era began! The union of the sexes has been made a blemish and a shame; merriment and

[50] *Les Gynographes* (p. 242) and *Le Pornographe* (p. 189) discuss nature as a moral realm of reality.

all that contributes to it a vice; pleasure, a crime. By fits morose and phil-anthropic, their crucified Christ . . . has wrapped all nature in the stuff of mourning and of bitter grief. . . . Sanction, oh, sanction pleasure, most sav-age lawgiver, it comes so rarely! [51]

Not even a slave could tolerate the unfounded denigration of life's "one real joy" that this so-called enlightened age fostered.

More cogent and more novel than his damnation of Christianity as the culprit, was Restif's analysis of love in civilization. First he characterized the emotion of love in Paris as bland, artificial, and weak. Love, "this first among all pleasures, this pleasure so pure . . . is only, in our cen-tury, a vague sentiment without energy. . . ." [52] It was bland because it was too easily gratified and had become satiated.

While other psychological theorists have seen civilization as overly repressive (for example, Freud in our own century), Restif felt that it was too free, that it imposed too few limits. [53] In a ballroom a group of coquettes aroused sensations that could not possibly be satisfied and were left choked and frustrated—they did not stimulate love but blunted its edge. In the unrestrained atmosphere of the cities, where all the arts and guiles of civilization were used to intensify sensuality too early in life, a frenetic pace of gratification ruined the tenderness of love, and turned its spontaneous expression into lust and cruelty. "Innocent affec-tion" was transformed into violent "savagery." A fancy wench passed into Restif's sight: "Her many graces, her figure, her voluptuous walk-ing . . . excited a perfect tempest of desires. . . . As had so often hap-pened, I forgot all other plans for the future: like a savage, I could see nothing but the immediate present." [54] When these overheated passions were fulfilled, impotence—actual physical weakness—resulted, not enjoy-ment: "the loss of vitality of the species in Paris is caused by exhaustian from overly excited pleasure. . . . excessive pleasure [is] incited by . . . the sensuality of adornment, erotic or overly-sentimental reading, in spectacles by the seasoned lures of actresses, by whores and the lewd provocations of coquettes. [55] Restif's condemnation was a sexual variation on Rousseau's theme that civilization increases desires without being able to fulfill them. (It is interesting to note that they both came to

[51] *Monsieur Nicolas,* Ellis edition, IV, 100.

[52] *L'Andrographe,* p. 24.

[53] The difference between Freud and Restif may be attributed at least in part to social conditions. Restif faced a sensual, aristocratic ruling class, while in Freud's time a Victorian bourgeoisie dominated society.

[54] *Monsieur Nicolas,* Ellis edition, II, 282.

[55] *Les Posthumes,* IV, 137.

Paris from puritanical backgrounds; Rousseau from Calvinist Geneva and Restif from Jansenist Burgundy.) People of culture, the wealthy who could afford it, were constantly exposed to sexual stimulation, Restif noted, resulting in a "vivacity" of the passions that was "dangerous." Their young were "precocious"; they were "prematurely" seeking love's pleasures. Ultimately, this process led to satiation, a loss for the individual of both attraction and desire.

Proceeding then from Restif's logic: if the passions provide the motive energy of life, and if sensual love is the fiercest passion of all, what can be said of civilized man who cannot properly feel and express this passionate nature? If he is drained of this primal energy through satiation what is the quality of his life? The appalling answers to these questions moved Restif to create his alter societies, his utopias.

What was the difference between the quality of love in utopia and in civilization? In utopia love was tender; it was a "divine feeling" that "spills out a sweet intoxication" and "permits us to tolerate the miseries of life and consoles us in the sad expectancy of death. . . ." [56] In civilization, where no effective controls for the passions existed, love "made man a ferocious animal," more "furious, more cruel than anger itself. It satisfied itself with gnashing teeth and murdered whatever it caressed!" [57] Restif's insight that civilization corrupts the passions, which are naturally good, would later be developed by Fourier and Saint-Simon with a much greater complexity. Restif's moralism would then be turned into a new psychology based on the passions.

D. RESTIF AND SADE

The ideals of love in the utopias of Restif and Sade provided alternative fantasies on a moral issue that plagued their generation. Was love purely natural or was it compatible with civilization? Could love become the basis of a secular ethic?

Restif and Sade knew of each other and read each other's books; they also treated each other with utter disdain. In the Bastille, when Sade's wife sent him some of Restif's books, he responded with an impassioned outburst of spleen.[58] Sade mentioned Restif twice in *Idées sur le roman*, both times with extreme distaste. "Restif de la Bretonne is flooding the public; he needs a press right at his bedside; fortunately, a single one

[56] *Le Pornographe*, p. 43.
[57] *Ibid.*
[58] Gilbert Lely, "Le Marquis de Sade et Rétif de la Bretonne," *Mercure de France*, No. 1130 (1957), pp. 364–366.

would groan under the burden of his dreadful output which is characterized by a low and prolix style, disgusting adventures which have been derived from the behavior of the worst kind of company and by no other merit for which any but the pepper merchants would thank him." [59] Since "the divine marquis" pulled social rank on Restif, it is interesting to note that allegedly the one time they met was while soliciting the same prostitute.

Restif was no less forthright. He recommended, with characteristic severity, that the publication of Sade's immoralities be suppressed and the author put to death.[60] The intensity of mutual abomination leads to the conclusion that each may have recognized in the other something of himself and was repulsed. On Restif's part, a dialectric of attraction/repulsion is dramatically evident in his late work L'Anti-Justine. Written expressly to negate the effect of Sade's hideous lewdness, to "disprove" Justine,[61] it ended as pure pornography, participating in the very "sadism" of Sade. If Justine connected love with pain and cruelty, L'Anti-Justine was intended to prove the opposite thesis: that love should be the result of pleasureful stimuli. Restif thus separated cruelty from lubricity except where he transparently parodied Sade.[62] The outright libertinage of L'Anti-Justine was coated with a thin layer of morality: the book, Restif reasoned, would stimulate married couples and thereby prevent adultery.[63] The plot, however, concerns the debauchery of a father with his daughters; L'Anti-Justine advertises incest, not the respectable forms of family love. Restif himself was not convinced of the morality of the book and never finished it or published it.[64] Restif's erotic sensibility together with his overt moralism led to a pathetic contradiction: he could neither resist Sade's sensuality nor fail to denounce it. He was both fascinated and horrified by pornography.[65]

The two writers had more in common than an interest in erotica; they belonged to the same generation. Sade was born in 1740, six years

[59] "The House of Sade," Yale French Studies, No. 35, p. 14. See also p. 16.

[60] Monsieur Nicolas, Ellis edition, VI, 181–183.

[61] Pleasures and Follies: L'Anti-Justine by Restif Bretonne [sic] (San Diego: Publisher's Export Co., 1967), pp. 1, 15–16. I have been unable to locate a French copy of L'Anti-Justine. The original edition is very rare. Due to current interest in pornography, several paperback editions have been published in this country. The one I have used appears to be a reprint of the recent Olympia Press translations.

[62] Ibid., pp. 145–151.

[63] Ibid., pp. 191–192.

[64] Childs, op. cit., p. 338.

[65] See Monsieur Nicolas, Ellis edition, IV, 242–244, where Restif recounts the effects pornography had on him.

after Restif, and died in 1814, eight years after him. Both spent long periods of solitude in contemplating the pleasures of sex. Sade, involuntarily caged in the Bastille, wrote novels to achieve a vicarious satisfaction in his characters' sensuality. Restif erected his own prison on the Ile Saint-Louis to relive his affairs by rereading signatures of passion he had inscribed on the walls. Sade yearned for the immediate gratification of his erotic needs, but Restif was sated by memories. On a quiet June night he would hunch near the wall and carve into it the name of a lover, some current business, a chapter completed, a dinner with friends, a fight with his wife. His chiseling done, he relaxed, letting his memory glide through moments of intense emotion by its own logic and momentum: back to duplicious Sara, to Louise and Thérèse, to the innocent Zéphire, to angelic Jeannette, to modest Edmée—soft, delicious moments, so pleasing to relive. Meanwhile, Sade planned new and more luscious tortures for Justine; a new position or a new justification.

Intellectually, the corrupted peasant and the effete nobleman reflected and shaped a new quality of the French sensibility. In each of their utopias, a fantasy of passion was played out on similar grounds but in different ways. There was the sharp awareness in both of an intimate connection between the instincts of love and aggression. Restif's perception of the destructive aspects of love has already been discussed: [66] Sade's needs no elucidation, since *La Philosophie dans le boudoir* spelled out a utopia of aggressive sexuality that immortalized his name in our vocabulary.

Both wrote copiously about the nature of love and its meaning for morality and civilization. Sade drove sensationalist psychology to its final reaches in the affirmation of crime as natural, necessary, and good. If nature was accepted as prescriptive, descriptive, or both, cruelty, so real a part of the passions, had to be legitimated. Love was the most natural of all pleasures, the surest source of happiness, and it had to be accepted in all its forms. Only hypocrites could deny the joys of flagellation, sodomy, homosexuality. Restif was taken aback by the argument. He saw and accepted the logic but denied the conclusions. Love was two-edged: it could be the source of either harmony or disorder in human relations. Sade was right to see in love the true foundation of happiness, but if every individual should try to gratify himself by destroying others, the result would be total annihilation. Therefore utopia of immediate, individual sexual fulfillment had to be rejected. In its place Restif proposed curtailed and channeled gratification for all. Love was expressed

[66] See also Crocker, *op. cit.*, p. 361.

as tenderness, as sympathy, as benevolence.[67] In Havelock Ellis's words, "Restif combined an extravagantly ostentatious anxiety for morality with an equally extravagant love for sexual license." [68] The result of this unlikely alliance was his utopia.

To understand how this mixture of ideas could be set forth as utopian, one must keep in mind the state of Parisian society, the horrors of which were symbolized by Sade himself. To Restif, love had become so mean, the veneer of civilization had worn so thin, Paris had regressed so near to animality, that drastic reforms were needed. "What is love among the fashionable people?—It is physical love debased beneath the sort resented by animals. . . . among fashionable people, it is a matter of caprice, a derangement of the imagination . . . it is a kind of uncivil swindle. . . ." [69] This was Restif's final word on Sade and the sensuality of the French aristocracy. Whereas Sade required a sophisticated apparatus of torture to incite his sensibility, Restif had only to catch a glimpse of a shapely ankle to arouse his primitive passions. The rude peasant condemned the polished lord; natural instinct denounced refined civilization.

From a perspective within civilization, Sade himself proclaimed that love was intrinsic to man's nature and criticized civilization as hypocritical in denying any of love's forms. He accepted the dynamic nature of the passions and carried his logic to perverse conclusions. Such courage (or cynicism) Restif did not have. His libertine self, confronted by the same aggressive passions as Sade, retreated into his Jansenist self. With the same force that Sade used to announce an ethic of torture, Restif postulated the socialization of the passions. Yet Restif's libertine self, exalting in love, could not be negated. Hence love required sublimation: the sensual act not only provided pleasure; it evoked the feeling of existence and gave life its meaning. This dialectic, running back and forth between an affirmation of love and the need for its renunciation, shaped love in Restif's utopia.

[67] Les Gynographes, pp. 250–251.
[68] From Rousseau to Proust (Boston: Houghton Mifflin, 1935), p. 172.
[69] Les Gynographes, p. 254.

IV

Work

A. TOWARD A NEW CONCEPT OF WORK

1. *The Worker and the Tradition*

Besides love, the other dominant activity and value in utopia was work. Restif did not articulate his utopia of love and work as well as the nineteenth-century utopians who followed him, but he did make broad outlines of the ideal.

In the elitist intellectual atmosphere of the Old Regime, Restif was perhaps more qualified than other utopians to plan the ideal organization of work—he had a varied workingman's background. His youth, in rural Burgundy, provided him with firsthand experience of the routine of the peasant: shepherding, planting and harvesting of crops, and everyday farm chores. After allowing him a short stint of schooling, Restif's father sent him to nearby Auxerre, a sizable town, to learn the craft of printing. He remained a printer, eventually becoming a foreman, until 1767 when his first book was published. The remainder of his life as a novelist and moralist involved him in the intellectual world. Thus Restif was no man of leisure.

In the French utopian tradition, the ideal of the Age of Gold was set against the reality of unending toil. An Edenic, pastoral image where nature's easy bounty made labor minimal enough to be untiring had haunted the French imagination since the seventeenth century. Fénelon's Bétique, one of the two major utopias in *Les Aventures de Télémaque*, revivified the dream of the Age of Gold and was one of the most popular books of the eighteenth century. In Bétique, wine flowed in the rivers and a benign, cornucopial nature protected man from the necessity of work. Still, for Fénelon work was hardly a blessing, and a mystical life

51

of contemplation was the ideal of the utopians. To minimize work in order to render it agreeable was their dream. In sharp opposition to the aristocratic scorn for work and the pastoral ideal of minimal effort, Restif presented work as the most useful function of man.[1] Work played an important role in utopia since it was an expression of the passions.

2. The Value of Work

Restif's concept of work was specifically directed against the contemporary values of aristocratic leisure and monkish contemplation. Freedom was not achieved by avoiding work; idleness did not lead to the repose and happiness of the soul. Only by submission to the discipline of work could the body and the mind be satisfied. In the following passage work appears as a good in itself, a direct source of happiness, although it has a different meaning at each stage in the life cycle.

. . . from infancy, man must envisage work as a means of repose. Then he will always be content; in the vigor of youth by pleasure and by the hope of being a man; in adulthood by the remembrance of his work (the badges he earned, the pleasures of his skill, the delight in his honors). Here, I believe, is the only means of making man happy.[2]

Youths enjoyed work in utopia as a pleasureful release of energy; adults as the satisfaction of accomplishment; elders as the memory of past fulfillment.

The philosophes were inteersted in the idea of work for another reason. In the Encyclopédie Diderot, noting the contributions of the crafts in man's progress, condemned the prevalent attitude of scorn for them, especially the educated man's complete ignorance of craft industries. He believed the inventions of artisans provided the keys to the advancement of human society.[3] The need of society was to conquer the traditional secretiveness of artisans and to disseminate the inventions of each group throughout every industry. Improvement in technology was a project of immense importance. The prints in the Encyclopédie, depicting machines and craft processes, were intended to give an impetus to interest in technology. Diderot's main intention was to make technology more efficient and bring an experimental and scientific spirit

---

[1] This has been noted by Maxime Leroy, Histoire des idées sociales en France de Montesquieu à Robespierre (Paris: Gallimard, 1946), I, 242.

[2] L'Andrographe, p. 173.

[3] Encyclopedia, trans. by Hoyt and T. Cassirer (New York: Library of the Liberal Arts, 1965), p. 6.

into the workshop. Nowhere in his article on "Art," however, was there an interest in the subjective experience of work; only the objective fact of efficiency was important to Diderot.

Restif, on the other hand, related the social function of work to the importance of the passions in work. But unlike Fourier, who saw work as a voluntary expression of various passions, Restif was interested only in the use of the passions as energy in work. Therefore, the rule in utopia was that everyone must work. "A being in society who does nothing is a monster, to whom everything is refused."[4] Idleness and leisure were sins. Work was not so much man's privilege as it was his obligation. On Christine Island, in *La Découverte australe par un homme volant*, the flying man established an ideal society where "the law of work was general, indispensable; useful occupation alone honored, idleness declared disgraceful. It became the mark of opprobrium and of degradation."[5] (The nineteenth-century sense of an attack on unemployment as an evil of capitalism must not be read into Restif's "law of work" or "right to work." His rule was directed at the laziness of the worker, not at the injustices of the economic system.)

"The law of work is a natural right [*droit*] for social man."[6] Contrary to the view of Helvétius and other social utilitarians, it was not society that determined man's nature, but man (and specifically man's need to work) that determined the nature of society. To Restif work was both natural to man and a matter of social obligation: it was imparted by nature and developed in society. Usually, when Restif wrote of man and work in utopia, he refused equally the position that man was by nature good and society artificial, and the view that man was by nature amoral and society the necessary moralizer. By stressing both the natural and the social, he attempted to reinforce the significance of work.[7]

A distillation of Restif's theories on work in utopia, however, reveals a very negative attitude—idleness is the great evil. What Restif feared from idleness was to a large extent the misuse of the passions. Very often a touch of the traditional notion that busy bodies make no trouble was prominent in his concept of work. For example, Restif ascribed the "atrocious behavior" of "clerks and those who are what is known as skilled workers" to the fact that "the work these young men do is not

[4] *Les Gynographes*, p. 202.
[5] *La Découverte australe*, II, 346; see also *Monsieur Nicolas*, Pauvert edition, VI, 87.
[6] *Les Gynographes*, p. 202.
[7] Note also that in contradiction to the whole thrust of the utopian writings, Restif, in *Les Posthumes* (I, 184), declared work and death "the greatest evils of life."

fatiguing, and it leaves the body with all its energy intact." [8] The natural right of man to work meant that work insured social order by exhausting the workers.

The most astonishing aspect of Restif's idea of "the law of work" is the lack of recognition that man's reason determines what work he shall do and the manner and extent to which he will do it. By obscuring the demarcation between society and nature Restif inevitably overlooked the individual's capacity to determine his own vocation. Individual commitment and a sense of calling are omitted in his idea of work. Restif merely assumed that a man would take up his father's occupation. The right to work meant only the necessity of doing something incessantly; the state would take care of those who did not work.

Diverging from the mainstream of the Enlightment, Restif did not relate work to progress or social evolution, did not attempt to justify work in terms of the future happiness of mankind. For him work was related only to the individual's present happiness and the general welfare of society. Progress in techniques of production and distribution did not appear to him as a cumulative phenomenon with untold significance for the future of man.

3. Idleness and the Organization of Work

Restif's notion of the nature of work was very uncomplicated. Instead of dividing work into distinct, exclusive, and hierarchical categories, he saw all work in utopia as one undifferentiated field of activity. Farming, crafts, the arts and sciences were merely different modes of participation in the same general activity. Restif was not immune to the temptation to erect hierarchies,[9] but on the subject of work he was more concerned with providing a general structure to regulate all work. The idea that work in itself was more important than its specific form enabled Restif to set it against its alternatives; thus he recognized what Leroy called the main social problem of the eighteenth century: beggars, or more generally, the unemployed.

In Le Thesmographe Restif reprinted an essay by Monthinot, devoted to mendicants, that approached the issue in a detailed and comprehensive manner.[10] Several distinct categories of unemployment were specified and

[8] Les Nuits de Paris, Barzun edition, p. 42.

[9] See, for example, the elaborate ranking of men of letters in L'Andrographe, pp. 185–186, and a system of ranking by productivity in Le Thesmographe, p. 108.

[10] I have not been able to determine whether or not the essay was actually written by Monthinot, who was a friend of Restif in the Grimod de la Reynière circle (Mes Inscriptions, pp. 105, 185).

each was subjected to separate consideration by the utopian legislator. Idleness and begging were not considered crimes in themselves, but vagabonds who refused to work out of laziness were to be punished by arrest and deportation to the colonies.[11] On the other hand, those who begged because they could not find work or were too old or disabled would be given aid by the government [12]—the existing system of poorhouses was abandoned as inhumane and inefficient. The goal of society was to find employment for those who could work and provide a decent existence to those who could not.[13] To condemn those on relief to the squalor of the poorhouse merely made it impossible for them to return to the work force. "The incapable poor must all be given work. . . . The handicapped poor must be put to public work. . . ." [14] The state must play a major role in providing work because man cannot control his fate, a fate that often distributes hardships unequally. "In the lottery of human life the worker is exposed to the hazards of misfortune. Lack of work, sickness, accidents, intemperance of the seasons all weigh upon him in the strongest manner." [15] In Ancient Sparta, Restif complained, "where only Helots worked, the Helot came to hate work. . . ." [16] To maintain for all a sense of dignity in their work, all utopians were integrated into a monolithic system. "Tasks are divided among all citizens, in proportion to strength and capacity, by the Elder-syndic of each neighborhood." [17] Characteristically, Restif drew up projects to cover all situations. Women of all social positions [18] were alloted certain duties, and even philosophers had to work four hours a day.[19] From youth until the ripe old utopian age of 150, everyone worked.[20]

The amount of work prescribed varied in each utopia. Generally, Restif reproduced the existing work hours. What was important, however, was not the number of hours but the rigidity of the work schedule.[21] Regulation was required because workers were like savages: as soon as they received their wages they went on a spree and did not return to work until their money was used up. Restif did not express

[11] *Le Thesmographe*, pp. 557, 573, 580.
[12] *Ibid.*, p. 562.
[13] *Ibid.*, pp. 570–573.
[14] *Monsieur Nicolas*, Pauvert edition, VI, 86.
[15] *Le Thesmographe*, p. 559
[16] *La Découverte australe*, II, 346.
[17] *Ibid.*, III, 499.
[18] *Les Gynographes*, p. 121.
[19] *La Découverte australe*, III, 514–516.
[20] *Ibid.*, III, 499.
[21] *L'Andrographe*, pp. 96–99, 171.

sympathy for his compatriots by an attack on working conditions or denunciation of the low level of wages; on the contrary, he demanded that they be kept at their jobs the whole week.

I reflected on the impropriety of the high price of handicrafts; I considered the pernicious consequences on the populace, who, like savage hordes, see only the present. If it can earn its necessities in there days, it works only three days and turns to debauchery the other four. But then it has no more necessities; it is miserable; it borrows, does not pay, ruins the baker, the shoemaker, the wine merchant. . . . All is in disorder. Instead of this, keep the price of handicrafts low. The populace, really a machine, will work like a machine six days a week, because it will need this work to meet its expenses. It will not throw itself into disorder, and will be less encumbered with debt. . . .[22]

The harsh tones of this passage are typical of his attitude toward work and workers. In utopia, the craft workers would be disciplined to work at the steady pace of the peasants. Nevertheless, in some of his moods, Restif was less repressive. Anticipating Fourier, he even permitted multiple occupations for the Megapatagons, they could change jobs at will.[23]

B. THE ETHICS OF EQUALITY

The principle which underlay the distribution of jobs and goods was not economic equality but merit. Not all men were paid the same because not all men had equal capacities. Once all utopians were busy, the problem shifted from individual fulfillment to social utility, in which a merit system of compensation was designed to obtain the highest productivity possible. Approbation was used as an incentive to stimulate the economy. Public acclaim, badges of distinction, and a vast hierarchy of honors and monetary differences were established to reward outstanding accomplishment. Restif ridiculed Rousseau for advancing "Jacobin equality, without regard to merit." [24]

Although Restif believed that work should be rewarded he was not convinced of the merit of a corollary idea—the right to private property. Restif joined the communists in calling private property a poor social institution. A strong sense of animosity against the rich pervaded Restif's works. A printer who was often out of work and poverty stricken, a writer who frequently received little compensation for his books even when they sold well, then a successful novelist who lost a comfortable

[22] Les Nuits de Paris, Boussel edition, pp. 11–12.
[23] La Découverte australe, III, 500–501.
[24] Monsieur Nicolas, Pauvert edition, VI, 393.

income by the inflation of *assignats*, Restif could hardly avoid a feeling of bitter indignation at the practices of those who enjoyed wealth and comfort, especially because in his eyes they were no better men than he. Add to this the countless little indignities suffered at the hands of the wealthy in everyday life and the case against private property must have seemed to him incontestable.

In the utopian tradition, the notion of a community of goods went back to Plato and More and was continued by most French utopians in the seventeenth and eighteenth centuries. J. H. Hexter has pointed out that this primitive communism resembled the moralists' attack on luxury, pride, and vice in general, more than the economic arguments of the nineteenth-century socialists.[25] To understand Restif's communism it is more propitious to look back to Lycurgus than forward to Marx. Lycurgus came to Restif through Plutarch and served as the model of the austere legislator. Plutarch's legendary account suggested that private possessions caused distempers in the veins of the body politic.[26] The "evils of insolence, envy, avarice and luxury" were inherent in riches. In order to obtain a virtuous citizenry, Restif agreed, private property had to be abolished. Communal property was advocated in *Les Gynographes*, *L'Andrographe*, *Le Thesmographe*, most of the utopias in *La Découverte australe par un homme volant*, and in the numerous little "plans of association" that punctuated Restif's novels. The crucial criterion in all of Restif's utopias was size. In the small community in France called Le Mont-inaccessible, private property could be abolished because all members of the community knew each other and were directly dependent upon each other.[27] In such a situation a fraternal atmosphere was easily established and incentives of property could be replaced by incentives of friendship.

The few pages of regulations called "Statuts du Bourg d'Oudun" demonstrate the moral nature of Restif's attack on property. Oudun was the most egalitarian of Restif's utopias. Hardly any property was individually owned: all land was divided into equal parcels, each family receiving an equal share. In the tiny village of twenty-five families, all distinctions were banned. To understand Restif's purpose it must be remembered that the model laws came at the conclusion of *Le Paysan perverti*. The reader had just been told the story of a peasant boy, Edmond Rameau, who

[25] *More's Utopia: the Biography of an Idea* (New York: Harper Torchbook, 1965), pp. 66–97. For a different view, see Leroy, *op. cit.*

[26] *Plutarch's Lives*, trans. by J. and W. Langhorne (New York: Mentor, 1964), p. 16.

[27] *La Découverte australe*, I, 141.

went to Paris and fell into evil ways.[28] The "Statuts" were intended to create a society that would prevent Edmond's fall—a society in which the family would act as a unit to protect its members.

> Considering that the sojourn in the city is dangerous for morals, we have resolved to prohibit it forever to all members of the family of R** who have not yet been there. In order to succeed at this, all of us, brothers and brothers-in-law, have established in concert a family pact which all our descendents will be obliged to observe under pain of disinheritance. . . .[29]

The aim of the egalitarian legislation was moral: to prevent villagers from leaving home and being exposed to the vices of Paris. Luxury, egoism, and private property were the corrupting influences. If, in fact, the village were made a true community, the motives for leaving would disappear forever.

The moral quality of Restif's attack on private property may also be illustrated by the epigraph to *L'Andrographe*, taken from Rousseau: "Cursed is he who was the first to enclose a common field, saying, 'this field is mine.' " Emphasis falls on the first word and the last word of the sentence, an emphasis that separates Restif from the socialists of the nineteenth century. A man who made property into a private possession was "cursed." The stress was on the moral evil of the economic act. Furthermore, the sin did not reside in the economic nature of the private possession of property, but in the willful act of "saying this field is *mine*." The egoism of a private-property economy was what Rousseau and Restif abhorred.

Unlike Voltaire, Saint Lambert,[30] the Physiocrats, and others who argued that luxury was necessary to civilization, Restif found it the source of many social evils; above all, it tended to isolate man from his fellows. Scorn and hate replaced love and esteem for one's neighbor.[31]

> . . . luxury is a monster which squanders surpluses to the fancy of spoiled children and denies necessities to those in need. It is luxury which gobbles up all that could be spent commendably and makes the richest poor in their opulence. It makes people callous, egotistical, greedy, knavish and forces, besides, so many women to sell their honor.[32]

---

[28] *Le Paysan perverti,* II, 335.

[29] *Ibid.,* p. 337.

[30] *Essai sur le luxe* (n.p., 1764), p. 17. The same article was printed in the *Encyclopédie*.

[31] *Le Thesmographe,* p. 412.

[32] *Les Gynographes,* p. 113.

Quesnay, Dupont de Nemours, and Turgot were mistaken, according to Restif, to see property as the basis of society, for it was destructive of human relations. Their doctrine permitted too much freedom in areas where men interact, assuming, for example, that "the so-called proprietor was the master of pricing his things as he wishes; that he could lose them, destroy them, give them to a foreigner without regard for shortages, the needs of his fellow citizens, or their poverty!" [33] Restif also charged that luxury destroyed the social nature of work. Whatever happiness man could obtain from his labor was lost because men were set in opposition to other men and became isolated and antagonistic to one another.[34] Part of the meaning of work lay in its ability to relate men to one another in a common enterprise; private property led only to "fraud, theft and murder." [35]

The utopian economic problem was to avoid the need for private property and luxury by creating a well-balanced system of rewards for merit. Exclusive interests were permissible only to the extent that society was not endangered.[36] The ideal was to have "everyone a possessor, but no one a proprietor." [37] Utopians could own things, but they could not do with them as they wished to the exclusion of consideration for the needs of their brothers. To obtain a just balance of individual and social interests the state had to play a major role in the economy, collecting and distributing all goods.[38] Since Restif viewed the economy primarily in terms of agriculture, the bureaucratic needs of his state were few. With trade and craft industries serving secondary functions, utopia had an economy of limited productivity. In this important respect its ideals differed from the dynamic economic ideals of nineteenth-century socialism. Restif's utopia avoided the vices of private property because it lacked incentives for economic progress and expansion. Without Saint-Simon's vision of an industrial society, it did not demand great economic risks and adventures. Since the economy was static, the little incentive that was necessary could be stimulated without causing great inequalities of wealth.

Wheat (or grain) was the pivot of the entire French economy in Restif's day. If the crop was good the people were fed and France was

[33] *Monsieur Nicolas*, Pauvert edition, VI, 55–56.
[34] *Ibid.*, VI, 309, 384; *La Découverte australe*, IV, 47.
[35] *Monsieur Nicolas*, Pauvert edition, VI, 310.
[36] *Le Thesmographe*, p. 121.
[37] *Ibid.*, p. 478.
[38] *L'Andrographe*, p. 103.

prosperous; if a blight destroyed the crop, prices rose and many went hungry or starved. What should the government's role be with respect to bread? The Physiocrats demanded the abolition of all feudal restrictions, such as tolls and prohibitions on imports between provinces, which inhibited the free movement of grains. In 1774, Turgot carried out these reforms with unfortunate results. Another group of publicists proposed that the price of grains be controlled by the state. A theorist whom Restif knew, Linguet, in *Théorie du loix civiles* (1767), insisted that a high price for grains intensified the misery of the poor: luxury was extracted from the toil of the people and a free economy only meant higher prices and more starvation, not higher wages as the Physiocrats claimed. Restif joined Linguet in providing for the regulation of the price of staples by the utopian municipality.[39] Furthermore, "All products will be put in common; fields, wines, meadows, beasts of all kinds, as well as products of crafts, arts and sciences." [40] No longer would three-fourths of the population work in slavery while the rest gorged themselves in comfort.

Compared to the state of the young science of political economy, Restif's understanding of the economy as a whole was rudimentary. Storage bins to preserve surplus grains and some "Committees" and "Bureaus" to regulate distribution were the extent of it. He could not rid himself of the belief that the economy could be equated with farming. Debt financing, foreign trade, colonial resources, industry, the laws of the marketplace, of supply and demand—these were beyond his ken. The wealth of nations denoted to him neither more nor less than a good crop and efficient agricultural techniques. In Chadourne's words, "This was not dialectical materialism. Significantly, it was on the ancient peasant tradition of patriarchy, of mutual aid and of community that the ideologue based himself in order to build a new order on the old." [41]

C. Work and Play

No revaluation of work in utopia could obscure the simple fact that the consistent application of man to his work, regardless of its dignity and worth, reduced that work to drudgery. The utopian fantasy had to account for the inevitable, recurrent disillusionment with work. Thus Restif made sure that escape from the grinding wear of man's dependence

---

[39] *Le Thesmographe*, p. 106.

[40] *Monsieur Nicolas*, Pauvert edition, VI, 311.

[41] Marc Chadourne, *Restif de la Bretonne, ou Le Siècle prophétique* (Paris: Hachette, 1958), p. 210.

on nature was provided by play. *Homo ludens* and *homo laborans* were poles between which Restif sought an ideal equilibrium. Too much play threatened the seriousness of work; too much work ruined the enjoyment of accomplishment. This connection between work and play was crucial to Restif's idea of work, for his thesis that work must use and involve the passions depended on it, and in order for work to be passionate it had to be interesting. If work itself was only another form of play then diversions and amusements were unnecessary; if work was not at all play then utopia must divert man from his constant toil and rejuvenate his passions by an assortment of amusements.

Juggling to find the balance of work and play best suited to the nature of man, Restif tried different formulas in different utopias. Where the rule of work was most strict and coercive, play became completely distinguished from work. Play in *L'Andrographe* was a reward for the toil of labor: "The rigorous imposition of work . . . will be compensated by days of rest and of pleasure during which everyone will enjoy equally diversions, public spectacles, etc." [42] In Megapatagonia, a better balance between work and play was projected. Restif argued that nature could provide for all man's needs without any great expenditure of collective effort, so long as all utopians worked: "When everyone works the pain is nothing; on the contrary, work is then only a pleasure because whatever the task an individual has, it never ends in fatigue. . . ." [43] There was another more radical possibility in Restif's dream: work and play could become one and the same thing: "work is almost a game, and the games are instruction. Every day is a holiday, but not as in Europe . . . there, one part of the human race diverted itself without doing anything, while the other worked without any diversion." [44] Finally, Restif philosophized that work was not a necessary part of man's nature. The polarity was broken and only *homo ludens* remained: "Man is not born to work; no being in nature is made for work, but for play, for amusement." [45] To the obvious retort that animals do in fact work, he replied that the building of a nest by a bird was not work but "an instinct of subsistence, propagation, pleasure." [46] Work was a passion, like love, and it was connected to the function of reproduction. Therefore, it had to be pleasureful, like the sex act. When he dissolved work into the biological process, Restif approached Fourier's "system of passionate attraction." Work,

[42] *L'Andrographe*, p. 98.
[43] *La Découverte australe*, III, 497.
[44] *Ibid.*, III, 503.
[45] *Monsieur Nicolas*, Pauvert edition, VI, 407.
[46] *Ibid.*

love and play were bound together; all were releases of energy, and all expressions of the passions were enjoyable.

If nature and society are substituted for play and work the full drama of Restif's thought emerges. The constant search for the right balance of work and play paralleled the central dilemma of his utopian thought. Was man to be civilized and made moral by permitting him to play in nature's garden, or by imposing upon him a society of work? It seemed that only a never-stabilized balance could make man moral. This was precisely the difficulty Restif sought to overcome.

The cycle of utopian life in *L'Andrographe* provided adequately but not plentifully for diversions from a routine of labor. Coming once each season, marriages were the most splendid festivals of that life. Sundays and two weekday afternoons were proclaimed time of repose. Memorable occasions familiar to the Old Regime, like the birth of a Prince, warranted a holiday.[47] During these rejoicings, the youths would entertain their elders with songs, skits, and a variety of games.[48] The tone of these amusements was decidedly akin to those of traditional rural life, with the whole community joining in the revelry.

D. THE SPECTACLES

Restif also planned for the needs of more literate city dwellers. A reformed Academy was designed to stimulate writing and reading for higher tastes. Above all, drama was the dominant form of utopian diversion. Restif was an avid theatergoer in Paris and he devoted an entire volume of the *Idées singulières, La Mimographe*, to the reform of "spectacles." [49] The debate over the effect of plays on public morality was intense in the eighteenth century. In the three major playhouses— *Opéra, Comedie italienne*, and *Comedie française*—moralists were free to criticize society and lampoon the Government's arbitrary controls. Since the companies were in the King's hands, or in the more frivolous hands of his current mistress, they shared the haphazard nature of Old Regime politics. During performances arrogant young aristocrats could create havoc with impunity. The language in the theater, the behavior of actors and actresses and their costumes, the construction of the houses, all contributed to the view that drama did nothing to polish the man-

---

[47] *L'Andrographe*, p. 99.

[48] *Ibid.*, p. 102.

[49] Paralleling the imaginary fate of *Le Pornographe, La Mimographe*, in Restif's mind, was adopted by Prince Martin Lubomirski of Poland. See Adolphe Tabarant, *Le Vrai visage de Réstif de la Bretonne* (Paris: Editions Montaigne, 1936), p. 163.

ners of Frenchmen; rather it encouraged rudeness. The literary scholar
F. C. Green has commented:

The morals of the *filles d'Opéra* of this period are a byword. . . . the actresses were almost without exception kept by noblemen or financiers, who
protected them against the management. . . . From all accounts the spec-
tacle which attracted audiences to the *Opéra* in the eighteenth century was
that which to-day appeals to the foreign clientèle of the *Folies-Bergères*.[50]

Restif's experience corroborated this account. He was once invited to a
party given by actresses which, before long, had degenerated into an
orgy, with the police coming to restore order. Critics of civilized morality were not likely to overlook the vices of the theater.

More inclined to see virtue as a social quality, Restif took exception
to Rousseau's assault. Drama was indeed moral, but not by a tendentious

Rousseau saw the theater as the epitome of civilized mores and consequently as a deleterious influence on morality. In *Lettre à D'Alembert
sur les spectacles*, denouncing D'Alembert for wishing to contaminate
Geneva with a comic theater, he asserted that plays do not instruct but
only amuse, do not purge the passions but excite them, do not foster a
moral sense but turn it into a frivolous game. "The theater, I am told,
managed as it should be, makes virtue lovable and vice odious. What's
that! Before there were comedies, were not good people loved? Were
not evil people hated?" [51] The sublimities of Corneille and Racine, the
wit of Molière, the power of Shakespeare—these marvels of complex
consciousness were lightly written off by Rousseau. The theater was
yet another artificial ruse of civilization, destroying the natural goodness of man's heart by its frivolity.

More inclined to see virtue as a social quality, Restif took exception
to Rousseau's assault. Drama was indeed moral, but not by a tendentious
praise of virtue and blame of vice; rather because it mirrored humanity
in all its poses. Agreeing with Mercier, his frequent partner at the theater,
Restif saw drama as a school for manners.[52] When a play represented
exactly what happened and in the manner that it happened, it touched
nature—it captured and persuaded. Each spectator could tell himself
with Menander, "I am a man. Everything I see here treats of humanity
and cannot be foreign or indifferent to me." [53] Plays were "the great
moral mirror" of the relations of the two sexes. Granted that actresses

[50] F. C. Green, *Eighteenth-Century France* (New York: Appleton-Century-Crofts,
1931), p. 177.
[51] (Paris: Larousse, n.d.), pp. 82–83.
[52] Sébastien Mercier, *L'An 2440*, trans. by W. Hooper as *Memoirs of the Year Two
Thousand Five Hundred* (London: Robinson, 1772), I, 202.
[53] *La Mimographe*, p. 123.

were licentious, and that other aspects of the theater militated against healthy mores, these were amenable to reform. In fact, this was the purpose of *La Mimographe*. Once cleansed of its minor abuses, the theater, Restif promised, would help to civilize man. "Isolated, savage man is vicious without shame, without remorse. Man in society has a powerful spur toward loving honesty and beauty in the approbation of his fellow man." [54]

Bringing men together and having them watch their own actions on stage, the theater evoked morality by emulation. Already Restif knew Rousseau's counterattack: emulation did not enforce morality, but disrupted it. Not *amour de soi*, love of oneself, but *amour propre*, love of what one wants others to think of oneself, of a projected ego-image, resulted from emulation. If the theater did not encourage morality directly through emulation, a more roundabout procedure had to be presented to save the drama. The method Restif proposed was the meticulous regulation of everything connected with a performance: from the physical appearance of the theater and the costumes and makeup of the actors and actresses, to the content of the plays, everything came within the reformer's purview. Thus, Restif adopted his customary stance: morality was a product of the minute regulation of behavior. At the same time, the only justification for imposing restrictions was pleasure. A monstrous architecture of laws would transform the theater into a beacon of virtue and morality. In the last instance, the utility of the theater was amusement; but properly controlled pleasure became good conduct.

Restif's idea of a moral theater in utopia should not divert us from the basic meaning of the theater in terms of the continuum of work and play. For in the last resort Restif provided for numerous amusements, the theater among them, for his utopians. This meant that work itself was not play, that in order for man to release his passions in work there had to be frequent games to make man forget his work. Restif's argument was not that there were separate passions of work and of play; only work provided the source for the expression of passion. His thesis was rather that work by itself was not sufficiently interesting either to be called play or to evoke the passions.

E. WORK AND LOVE

Restif incorporated the values of both love and work into the mesh of utopian institutions through a series of regulations. He guaranteed the

[54] *Ibid.*, p. 80.

gratification of love and the fulfillment of work by an all-encompassing series of laws that curbed, limited, and hemmed in the passions. Obsessively, he permitted no gray areas of experience: there were no dark allys in utopia where love or work could get lost, go astray, or become corrupted. In a strange juxtaposition of attitudes, he adopted secular, flesh-and-blood values only to inhibit them by Calvinist, otherworldly denials. The sins in utopia were disorder, anarchy, insecurity, uncertainty. Salvation was found in a tight ordering of existence, of cubbyholing pleasure into safe, neat boxes of gratification. The most natural biological functions were sanctified by imposed value; but moral behavior was possible only in a society where nature was refashioned into the constricted patterns of Restif's fantasy.

Revolting against the aristocratic and Christian conceptions of social activity, Restif negated the values of contemplation, prayer, and honor. The philosopher, the monk, the soldier, and the courtier were not the models of man in the ideal society. The new way for man was found through love and work. Happiness, meaning, and order were derived from the new assessment of man's role.

These values, although with different contents, were taken up by the utopian socialists of the early nineteenth century. For Fourier and the Saint-Simonians, the relationship of love and work was a basic social problem. Endorsing a nonrepressive society that accepted and gratified the passions, Fourier did not find love and work antagonistic. Both were human passions and both were equally valid endeavors. The prejudice that love was frivolous and work alone was serious had no foundation from the perspective of the passions. "Love in phalanstery is no longer, as it is with us, recreation which detracts from work; on the contrary it is the soul and the vehicle, the mainspring of all works and of the whole of universal attraction." [55] The order of love and the order of work were integrated and dissolved in the system of "passionate attraction."

Restif's conception of the relation of love and work did not have the clarity and force of Fourier's. Only dimly did he formulate man's vocation in terms of love and work. He must be placed at the beginning of this trend in utopian thought, before the main lines of concern were clarified. Nevertheless, Restif treated love and work as basic social questions, involving the passions, and his manner of handling each was similar. Whereas Fourier opted for the free expression of the passions in

[55] Frank Manuel, *The Prophets of Paris* (New York: Harper Torchbook, 1962), p. 214.

multiple forms of love and work, Restif sought to place severe restrictions on both. Everyone must work and everyone must marry; everyone worked during the prescribed hours and everyone loved only his wife. The similarities and contrasts of these utopians offer a unique comparison in the history of the European fantasy. Restif and Fourier dreamed of an ideal life pattern consisting of man's absorption in love and work without much emphasis on reason. What for Fourier was a direct expression of the passions was for Restif a matter of their repression by society. There is no trace, in either of them, of the control and direction of man's work and love by his own unaided reason. The opposite formulations of Restif and Fourier indicate that the eighteenth-century view of man as a rational, social animal, who could be restricted by external law with relative ease because he could see the utility of these laws by his reason, was no longer secure. If the desire of the utopians was for either total regulation or no regulation at all, basic premises about the relation of man's passions to social needs became problematical. Thus the utopias of love and work pointed to a new level of questioning about the moral nature of man.

V

Social Structure

A. FRENCH SOCIETY

The Fournier printing plant, where Restif served his apprenticeship, bore all the marks of French society as a whole. When he arrived in Auxerre he took the lowest status among the apprentices, and the most menial jobs fell his way. But his father knew M. Fournier, the owner, and all the workmen understood Restif's privileged position. Madame Fournier liked Restif, so his position in the household was higher than that of most journeymen. Among the local girls he gained favor and enjoyed the benefits of his charm and appearance. Thus, confronting Restif was a series of social groups in which his position was different in each one. The mere fact of his birth to a well-off peasant did not fully determine his social position.

Eighteenth-century France was a hierarchical society in which social mobility was restricted by one's birthright. The vitality of the most strongly defined categories in the social structure, however, was waning and was continually called into question during the century. Accounts of the absurdities and injustices of the Old Regime are plentiful and need no retelling. What is pertinent to this study is the reaction of the utopians to the social system. The opposite of hierarchy is equality and equality became the dominant social principle of utopia as the century progressed. From the pleasant pastoral imagery of Fénelon's Bétique in 1699 to Babeuf's strident dogmas of the *Manifesto of the Equals* during the Directory, the principle of equality gained in intellectual and emotive force. To list the major utopias of the Old Regime is to list adherents, in one form or another, of equality. Vairesse, Foigny, Morelly, Rousseau, Mercier, Condorcet—the exception would only point up the rule. To assert that these utopians advocated equality is not enough. The nature, extent, quality, comprehensiveness, clarity, and force of the arguments must be considered. Here only Restif is under review.

B. "Statuts du Bourg d'Oudun" (1775) and "Les 20 épouses des 20 associés" (1780)

The best statement of the principle of equality in Restif's utopias can be found in "Statuts du Bourg d'Oudun." This short list of regulations has already been discussed in connection with Restif's notion of private property. Now Restif's plan for the ideal social organization is at issue. Oudun was, hypothetically, a small peasant village of not more than one hundred families. The life of the villagers revolved completely around the village, which provided for all their needs, spiritual and material. Each family owned an equal plot of land upon which it had "the rights of a lord without the title." [1] By placing all possession in the hands of the community as a whole, the rules prevented any single individual or family from attaining more goods than the next. The community also retained all authority since the elders of each family acted alternately as judges and administrators.[2] No nobleman, bishop, or officer of the central government could disturb the equality of the villagers, for wealth and social privileges simply did not exist.

Restif had a number of concrete sources from which to borrow ideas for Oudun. First, there was his own home, Sacy, although private property made it less than utopian. From Sacy he took an administrative system for Oudun, especially the assignment of important roles to the curé and the schoolmaster, who became responsible for the moral tone of Oudun.[3] Second, Restif fashioned his idea for an autonomous egalitarian community after several models, contemporary and historical. "La petite Sparte," [4] always an important model for Restif, was mistakenly conceived as an incarnation of Plato's *Republic*, as it was by many theorists in the eighteenth century.[5] The Guaranis, a Jesuit-controlled society in Paraguay, the Moravians of Lusace in Germany and the self-contained peasant families of Auvergne [6] were the more important existing models for Oudun. In an article in the *Encyclopédie* on

---

[1] *Le paysan perverti*, II, 338.

[2] *Ibid.*, II, 348.

[3] *Ibid.*, II, 342, 349, 352.

[4] *Ibid.*, II, 335, 339.

[5] R. Ruyer, *L'Utopie et les utopies* (Paris: Presses universitaires de France, 1950), p. 199. He mentions that *L'Esprit des lois* and Vairesse committed the same error.

[6] *Le Paysan perverti*, II, 335 and *Le Nouvel Emile*, I, 469–471, 474.

the Moravians, Faiguet characterized them as a "perfect society," where men lived in complete equality.[7] What attracted Restif in each of these societies was a sense of moral as well as physical equality that united individuals into families. All men were brothers—not in the abstract sense of belonging to humanity, but with the flesh and blood equality of a primitive tribe. Equality was not a matter of legal rights and obligations; it was a sense of intimacy between members of one cohesive community.[8] Hence Restif's concept of utopian social organization, in the first instance, was a variation on the timeless communitarian ideal.

In the forty-two volumes of novelettes about women called *Les Contemporaines*, Restif took out space to elaborate another small utopian community, this time for workers in Paris. It complemented the "Statuts du Bourg d'Oudun," the utopian community for peasants. Both town and country now had models of association to follow. Similar to Oudun's, this "plan of association" called for equality of wealth, social status, and authority, for only through equality could the association achieve the "intimacy" that was the basis of a moral community.[9] The location for the association was one city block and membership included the residents who voluntarily sought the compact for mutual security.[10] Members ranged in vocation from craftsmen and merchants to professional men. Significantly, all vocations represented a more or less similar social position. In eighteenth-century France, all would fall in the broad category of lower bourgeoisie (many professionals had not yet elevated their social status), so Restif did not really risk much by proposing equality among them. Although "Les 20 épouses des 20 associés" advocated a workingman's association of the mutual-aid type that later interested Proudhon, it was not economically based and did not aim toward power or a redistribution of the profits of enterprise, since it did not try to enlist all the members of a particular guild or vocation. In short it was clearly not a trade union or a *syndicat*. In one commentator's words, it was "a simple *mise en commun* of resources to gain strength in the struggle for life." [11]

[7] (Neuchatel, 1765), tome 10, pp. 704–706.

[8] E. Schmidt (*Der Idealstaat* [Berlin: Rüde, 1904]) and Hans Girsberger (*Der utopische Sozialismus des 18. Jahrhunderts in Frankreich und seine philosophischen und materiellen Grundlagen* [Zurich: Rascher, 1924], pp. 100–107) maintain that Restif was a precursor of socialism because he modeled his utopias after these communities.

[9] *Les Contemporaines*, II, 451.

[10] *Ibid.*, II, 394.

[11] B. Malon, "Rétif de la Bretonne," *Revue socialiste*, IX, No. 54 (June, 1889), 668. For interpretations of Restif's thought from a socialist orientation, see André

Yet Restif's inventiveness in formulating these miniature utopias of equality for both town and country foreshadowed the achievements of the utopian socialists of the early nineteenth century. In *Le Nouvel Emile* (1776), another peasant village for one hundred families was projected.[12] Town associations were drawn up in *Les Nuits de Paris* (1794) for thirty families and in *Le Nouvel Abeilard* (1778) for only four couples.[13] Restif's persistence in coupling equality with new forms of social organization calls for explanation. His social ideals have been compared with Fourier's in an attempt to show Restif's influence, but an unbridgeable gap exists between Fourier's attempts to base his Phalanstery on a perfect arrangement of psychological types and Restif's idea of brotherhood. Nowhere in Restif's utopias is there the brilliant if fantastic possibility of using social organization as an arena for the gratification of the unique psychic needs of each individual. Restif was never weaned from the eighteenth-century assumption that men were basically identical units in the social universe. Likewise, Restif's technique of communal housing had been anticipated by others.[14] Fourier's special uses of it cannot be attributed solely to Restif's influence.

In his use of the words "association" and "social" Restif came closer to the tradition of Rousseau and Mercier. Leroy, a historian of social thought, argued that Rousseau saw a new dimension of community, a phenomenon that could be termed "the social," which existed in addition to the king, the state, other authorities and other groups.[15] By "society" Rousseau meant a reality above individuals but one that held them together. Thus Rousseau intended to combat the philosophes' mechanistic image of society, in which men were atomically complete in themselves. This, to Rousseau, was the vice of egoism. Following him, other utopians like Mercier, in *L'An 2440*, shunned egoism and desired a society where men would "mutually assist each other." [16] Just this idea that all men

Lichtenberger, *Le Socialisme du XVIIIe Siècle* (Paris: Alcan, 1895), pp. 206–220; A. Ioannisiani, "L'Utopie de Restif de la Bretonne et le communisme utopique," *La Pensée* (March–April, 1958), pp. 91–103 (in general, Ioannisiani concentrates on *Monsieur Nicolas* and *Les Nuits de Paris*. He does not give thorough consideration to *Idées singulières*); F. Pringault, "Restif de la Bretonne communiste," *Mercure de France*, tome 106 (December 16, 1913), pp. 732–739.

[12] *Le Nouvel Emile*, IV, 45–48.

[13] *Les Nuits de Paris*, V, 966–968; *Le Nouvel Abeilard*, III, 336–341. Also see *La Découverte australe*, III, 481.

[14] See Bernard le Bovier de Fontenelle, *La République des philosophes, ou Histoire des Ajaoiens* (Geneva: n.p., 1768), p. 54.

[15] Maxime Leroy. *Histoire des idées sociales en France de Montesquieu à Robespierre* (Paris: Gallinard, 1946), I, 156–159.

[16] Sébastien Mercier, *L'An 2440*, trans. by W. Hooper as *Memoirs of the Year Two Thousand Five Hundred* (London: Robinson, 1772), pp. 160–161.

in a community were related to each other, regardless of differences in status or wealth, was the meaning of equality to Restif and the assumption of later utopian socialists. An organic picture of society in which all men were equal at the deepest level was Restif's intention in "Statuts du Bourg d'Oudun," "Les 20 épouses des 20 associés," and the other miniature plans of association.

"Statuts du Bourg d'Oudun" and "Les 20 épouses des 20 associés" fell specifically in a current of utopian thought connected with Rousseau's *Discours sur l'origine de l'inégalité* (1755). Rousseau's contrast between innocent, egalitarian, primitive societies and effete, hierarchic civilizations was a striking example of a trend that had begun with Fénelon's Bétique. By 1780, when Restif wrote, a long list of communitarian utopias, mostly in the imaginary-voyage genre, extolled the simplicity of a fictitious arcadia where the noble savage shared his property with his tribesmen and led a life that was both untrammeled and virtuous.[17] It would be difficult to overemphasize the popularity of these utopias in the French fantasy. Fénelon, *Les Aventures de Télémaque* (1699), Gilbert, *L'Histoire de l'isle de Caléjava* (1700), Gueudeville, *Dialogues ou entretiens entre un sauvage et le Baron de la Hontan* (1704), Tyssot de Patot, *Voyages et aventures de Jaques Massé* (1710), Morelly, *Naufrage des Isles Flottantes, ou Basiliade du célébre Pilpai* (1753), Tiphaigne de la Roche, *Histoire des Galligènes* (1765)—the list is barely begun. Each of these utopias transformed the Morean image of a society free of private property, avarice, and ambition into a land of calm felicity where the complex troubles of civilization vanished. Rousseau made the thesis of these utopias clear in his *Discours:* natural man was moral and civilized man was corrupt because the primitive society was established on the principle of equality. The purpose of these utopias was polemical and critical: France could be reformed on the egalitarian model of utopia. The desire for equality, expressed in the modes of fantasy, was symptomatic of a profound discomfort with the refinements of civilization and a wish to return to a perhaps mythic condition of simplicity, of an integrated emotional life, of a feeling of guiltless vitality. The communitarian utopias of the noble savage argued that an alternative path was open to man, the path of equality.

Elements of this primitivism in the utopian dream were prominent in Restif's Megapatagonia of 1781.[18] In contrast to Restif's other utopias,

---

[17] See Girsberger, *op. cit.;* Lichtenberger, *op. cit.;* Gilbert Chinard, *L'Amérique et le rêve exotique dans le littérature française au XVIIe et au XVIIIe siècle* (Paris: Hachette, 1913); René Gonnard, *La Légende du bon sauvage: contribution à l'étude des origines du socialisme* (Paris: Médicis, n.d.).

[18] *La Découverte australe*, III, 481.

only five regulations were required to establish this ideal society. Since the Megapatagons were unencumbered by civilization, they were natural, and therefore good. The laws that were imposed were only the basic postulates of the primitive, organic society of equals. First, the golden rule: "Be just toward your brothers; that is, ask for nothing except what you would want to give yourself, or do to others only that which you would wish done to yourself." (This variation on the primary rule of morality was reiterated throughout the century in different systems of secular morality and ended as Kant's universal maxim.) Second, "Be just toward animals, and in such a way that you would wish an animal superior to man to act toward you." The second moral law of Megapatagonia integrated man with nature to the extent that utopians behave ethically toward all beings on the earth. In Restif's eyes, man had a privileged position in the chain of being only if he deserved it, only if he was morally superior to the other creatures. Third, "Everything shall be communal among equals." By abolishing private property and eliminating the vices of civilization, the third law placed Megapatagonia in the current of communitarian utopias. Fourth, "Each works for the general good," and fifth, "Each participates in it equally." These two laws assured the permanent abolition of inequality and luxury, while formulating a division of labor and a distribution of wealth that achieved their permanent form in Marx's "From each according to his capacity; to each according to his needs." Restif's early version of the socialist tenet stressed the communal nature of work and a more absolute egalitarian system of distribution. The identification of the natural with the good, the abolition of property, the simplicity of laws and manners, the view of society as a brotherhood and the emphasis on the community over the individual were common features of the ideal society from Fénelon to Morelly.

Restif's uniqueness lay in experimenting with these principles in forms of community that were not faraway and exotic. "Statuts du Bourg d'Oudun" and "Les 20 épouses des 20 associés" brought the imaginary-voyage, egalitarian utopia to the French countryside and city. Restif tinkered with the social environment of the peasant and the craftsman, giving the utopian fantasy the aspect of reform by projecting the assumed innocence of the primitives onto the nature of the lower classes. Since the populace was viewed as not so very different a creature from the savage, the transformation was not difficult to conceive.[19] These

---

[19] In *The Natural History of Religion* (New York: Meridian, 1963), p. 51, Hume equated the primitive, anthropomorphic mind with that of the "vulgar" lower classes.

utopian projects [20] formed one step in the general movement of egalitarian social thought: from the exotic travel literature of the Renaissance, to the imaginary-voyage utopias of the eigheenth century (Megapatagonia), to the small plans of association, and finally to the utopian socialist works of the nineteenth century.[21] Thus the model member of the organic community of equals evolved from the Polynesian, to the imaginary noble savage, to the workingman. Restif's experiments with possible forms of association among small numbers of workers and peasants were an important contribution to this development.

C. THE EPIGENETIC CYCLE

It was typical of Restif not to be satisfied with one extreme statement of man's potentials: if equality was one ideal principle of society, inequality was another. In his effort to conceive a society of intimate fellowship where sympathy permeated human relationships, Restif went beyond the abolition of property and a return to the utopia of the noble savage to negate the principle of equality entirely. The moving principle of the natural society was not the abstract phantom of equality but the biological fact of age: his model was not the brotherhood but the patriarchal family—China, not Sparta.

The great non-Christian civilization of the East that caused so much debate in the eighteenth century [22] offered Restif an ideal manifestation of the seven ages of man. In China social relationships were governed by the same respect for age that Restif experienced in his youth. The chaos of Paris, where children laughed and hurled missiles of mud at Restif while he sought his peaceful escape beneath the walls of the Ile Saint-Louis, was overcome in China by the order of the epigenetic cycle. The wise Confucius was a model utopian legislator. To be sure, Restif was not much bothered by the accuracy of his image of paternal China. Travel reports gave conflicting judgments: men of commerce denounced the China they saw in dealing with native merchants; Jesuits

[20] Other plans of association resembling Restif's are discussed in Lichtenberger, *op. cit.*, pp. 325–357.

[21] See Gonnard, *op. cit.*

[22] The image of China in the eighteenth century has received noteworthy scholarly treatment, though the topic of the cultural confrontation of Europe and China is not well understood. There are two studies of particular interest, both including fine bibliographies: Virgile Pinot, *La Chine et la formation de l'esprit philosophique en France, 1640–1740* (Paris: Geuthner, 1932); and L. A. Maverick, *China, A Model for Europe* (San Antonio: Anderson, 1946) which includes a translation of Quesnay's *Le Despotisme de la Chine*. Also see Adolf Reichwein, *China and Europe: Intellectual and Artistic Contacts in the Eighteenth Century* (New York: Knopf, 1925).

exalted Chinese culture as it was presented to them by mandarins. Restif dismissed the ambiguities with a grand gesture of approval for a social system that made respect for age a cornerstone of moral conduct.

The standard that determined rights and obligations for utopians, in the first instance, was the epigenetic cycle: "Subordination will be graduated between all men from the age of three up to the age of one hundred, so that a child of three necessarily defers to one of four, and so forth. . . ." [23] Nothing disturbed him more than the philosophes' lack of respect for age. Inherent in their attack on traditional customs, Restif felt, was the desire to obliterate the natural order of ages. In 1657 Cyrano de Bergerac, whom Restif read, satirically portrayed a utopia where the distinction of age was reversed and children ruled their fathers. Youth, Cyrano contended, had "the power to imagine, judge and act"; certainly it was "more capable of ruling a family than an infirm sixty-year old. . . . " [24] To Restif, on the contrary, respect for age and deference to elders was the vital natural law of social organization. [25]

Since age also brought physical decay and a general drying up of sensibility, respect and authority became a consolation for the elders—a consolation of great value in a society that regarded sensual pleasure as the highest good and that provided no hope for a life after death. [26]

Restif's plan for a social order based on ranking by age was of course a means of satisfying man's need for authority. However, he emphasized the different needs of different age groups in an attempt to integrate the epigenetic cycle into the social structure. His intent—and his underlying rejection of an egalitarianism that failed to recognize what were to him concrete differences among men—must be seen in terms of the later utopian socialists, especially Fourier, who accentuated the richness and variety of humanity at the expense of the Enlightenment notion of the essential sameness and uniformity of man. The penchant of the eighteenth century to view all men as equal in rational capacity and different only as a result of the vicissitudes of experience and custom was rejected by Restif. Passion, which he believed was fundamental in man, was clearly subject to marked differences depending on age. Although he did not go as far as Fourier's different personality types, he anticipated the Romantic idea that love was only pure in youth and thus old age must find its gratifications in other spheres.

[23] L'Andrographe, p. 40.

[24] Other Worlds: The Comical History of the States and Empires of the Moon and the Sun, trans. by G. Strachan (London: Oxford University Press, 1965), p. 64.

[25] L'Andrographe, p. 13 of Preface.

[26] See ibid., pp. 16 of Preface, 15, 21; also La Découverte australe, III, 483; Monsieur Nicolas, Pauvert edition, VI, 323–324.

. . . in spite of fervent passions, we are virtuous in youth; we become less so as we reach maturity, while all physical and moral delicacy evaporates as we decline towards old age. If all old men are not blackguards, it is a matter of inertia rather than of principle. . . . For old men to be virtuous by inclination, age must be honoured and ambition and esteem produce the same effect as youthful sensibility and virile energy.[27]

Condillac's statue, with its capacity to receive sensations, was not a true model of man but rather a misleading fiction. The whole tradition of sensationalist psychology was in question because men could not be considered abstract, identical receptors of external stimuli. At each age, a man had a different capacity to feel, a different manner of being open to sensations. When Restif reintroduced the idea of authority in utopia he was not merely going back to the old-fashioned, pre-Enlightenment concept of social order. The nature of man's passions, not tradition, made a social hierarchy necessary.

Restif created sharp social boundaries based on age and gave to each category distinct duties and privileges.[28] Each category was given a title; infant, youth, adolescent, young-married, young-man, man, and so forth. Restif's aim was to make the passage from age to age as significant as it was biologically natural. The boundaries dividing age from age were sharpened and transitions were attended by appropriate rituals. Each age received more authority and responsibility than its immediate predecessor.[29] With characteristic diligence, Restif spelled out the specific qualities of each group through regulations which covered all aspects of the life cycle. "Young men" 35–49) had great capacities for activity. Still, only "Men" (49–59) could be public administrators as they were beyond the "greenness" of their juniors and had the necessary experience.[30] Women received a parallel set of rules [31] stressing both the differences among women and between them and men.[32] The tendency of these regulations was to delay the dignities as long as possible. For instance, one was not given the title "Man" until the age of forty-nine. Deferring gratification, as already noted in the chapter on love, was Restif's method of heightening expectation and rendering fulfillment more intense. It was also his response to what he considered an immoral habit of Parisians—giving too much freedom to their children too soon in life. Already, Restif warned, the effect of the permissive education of *Emile*

---

[27] *Monsieur Nicolas*, Ellis edition, VI, 111.
[28] *L'Andrographe*, p. 66.
[29] *Ibid.*, p. 166.
[30] *Ibid.*, p. 173.
[31] *La Découverte australe*, III, 555; *Les Gynographes*, p. 129.
[32] *L'Andrographe*, p. 67.

was at work in the metropolis. In his utopia, the capacities of each age received fresh consideration. Infancy and extreme old age were the most helpless; thus their duties were light and they were served by all other groups.[33] As the patriarchal family was breaking up and the individual began to be left completely on his own in large anonymous cities, Restif felt the need to provide for the elders of society. Youth was made responsible for the roughest physical labor and adults governed the society. With each age viewing the one above it with respect, and looking forward to its own power, the social structure, although sharply divided into categories, took on the character of interrelatedness and even unity. The individualistic, atomic society of the philosophes was replaced by the organic utopian world.

D. PATERNAL AUTHORITY

Related to Restif's concept of the epigenetic cycle was his idea of utopian society as a macrocosm of the individual family. "The state is a great family; each family is a small state. . . ."[34] In the ideal, organic society, the separateness of individuals was overcome by a "tie of connectedness among all members," an "adhesion that established a genuine togetherness."[35] The family served the same purpose in Restif's utopia as the general will did in Rousseau's *Contrat social:* it made for a cohesive society in which egoistic self-interest was overcome by a sense of intimacy with others, a feeling of sympathy for one's fellow man that Rousseau saw in the savage. But there were many kinds of families, many different systems of dominance, many different configurations of consanguinity that a family could embody.

There was no question to Restif about the nature of the ideal family; it was patriarchal. By no means was the patriarchal family a new principle of social organization in the utopian tradition. Some eighteenth-century utopians—Berington,[36] Moutonnet de Clairfons,[37] and Morelly [38]—had projected similar views. Furthermore, both Moutonnet and Morelly were communists. Like Restif, they coupled a community of goods, or economic equality, with a hierarchical social order based on the family.

---

[33] *La Découverte australe,* III, 551.

[34] *L'Anthropographe,* p. 22.

[35] *Le Nouvel Emile,* Bachelin edition, III, 199.

[36] In C. Garnier, ed., *Voyage imaginaries* (Amsterdam: n.p., 1787–1789), *Les Mémoires de G. de Luques,* X, 198–199.

[37] *Ibid., Les Isles Fortunées,* VI, 202, 205.

[38] Morelly, *Code de la nature, ou Le Véritable esprit de ses lois,* ed. by Chinard (Paris: Clavreuil, 1950), p. 204.

Thus the pattern combining equality and subordination in Restif's organization of society was not atypical. His superficially ambiguous statement, "The equality I ask for does not exclude subordination; on the contrary, it supposes that it is inviolable," [39] should now be comprehensible. The utopias of both Morelly and Restif resolved the struggle of all against all, "the habitual condition of enemy against enemy," [40] and achieved organic communities.

The models of society praised and adopted by Restif show the strength of his belief in the patriarchal family. Confucian China was high on his list of social ideals. "The political government of China is based on the mutual obligations of fathers and children. The emperor is the father of the state; a viceroy is the father of the province that he governs; a mandarin in the city that he commands." [41] The strongest model of the patriarch, however, was the Jew, the descendant of Abraham. In *La Vie de mon père* (1779), Restif recalled that Abraham and the book of Genesis were favorite reading at La Bretonne; that his father would read from Genesis to the whole family, inspiring respect.[42] The image of Abraham fused with his memory of his childhood and the Jew remained for him a perfect embodiment of the venerable traits of the benevolent patriarch. Late in his life, according to *Les Nuits de Paris*, Restif chanced upon a group of Jews in the Soubise Garden and the old memories were rekindled: "It seems that innocence and patriarchal morals still reigned among them. The maid servant spoke to her master and her mistress like a sister or a daughter, according to her age. The children were respectful and tender. The fathers and the mothers appeared to breathe only for them. I was edified by the sentiments of these poor Jews. . . ." [43] The force of his memories of the Old Testament was so strong that he quoted long passages in *Les Gynographes*.[44] After the Revolution had begun, Restif asserted that its basic cause was not the popular notion of the influence of "the writings of Voltaire and other philosophes," but "insubordination in the family." The remedy could only be "the most firm paternal authority." [45] It is interesting to note, in this connection, the relationship he saw between rebellion against society and rebellion against one's father—the revolu-

[39] *L'Andrographe*, p. 28.

[40] *Monsieur Nicolas*, Pauvert edition, VI, 423.

[41] *L'Andrographe*, p. 337. See also *Le Thesmographe*, pp. 162–164. Restif also viewed contemporary Denmark as a paternal state in *Le Thesmographe*, p. 272.

[42] P. 73.

[43] Boussel edition, p. 81.

[44] Pp. 130–146. 149–154.

[45] *Le Thesmographe*, p. 502.

tionaries were only little boys who had not been properly disciplined in youth. "Rebellion" of sons against fathers, which he rudely repressed in his utopia,[46] was the same evil as the Revolution of 1789, only in different clothes.

To institute a patriarchal social order, the absolute authority of the father in the household had to go unquestioned. "As soon as he enters the household, the husband will have a plenitude of power over his family. . . . " [47] To further secure this authority an endless series of rules covered all situations of daily life. For example, women sat across from their husbands during dinner and were not allowed to speak.[48] Again, Restif carried his restrictions beyond the patriarchal utopia of Morelly in *Code de la nature*. In fact, the authority of the patriarch was so satisfactory a means of social control that all institutions of reward and punishment were given a distinct familial tone. The Moral Register, the Committees of Women, and the Committees of Criminal Justice [49] all executed their authority not like impersonal bureaucracies but like severe fathers and mothers.

The State as well bore the stamp of paternalism. Restif expanded seventeenth-century absolutism by extending the areas of the State's responsibility for its citizens. Each town and village was provided with a public hospital featuring a separate room for each patient and nurses who consoled him with tenderness.[50] Cities were also in need of the reformer's attention. As traffic and reckless driving were great problems, the number of carriages was limited and galloping in crowded streets forbidden.[51] Restif had witnessed many cruel scenes where drivers would not stop even after downing a pedestrian.[52] Then too, a system of garbage disposal was needed to prevent epidemics and to freshen the air.[53] Industries that produced foul stenches would have to be relocated outside populous cities.[54] In the role of city planner Restif saw the advantages of reform from above: only a paternal government could correct endemic social disorders. It was in its tone especially that the utopian state displayed paternal qualities. More fatherly than legalistic, it brought justice and security to its citizens with a kind but firm hand. No one

---

[46] *L'Andrographe*, p. 40.
[47] *Ibid.*, p. 165. See also p. 69.
[48] *Monsieur Nicolas*, Pauvert edition, VI, 393–394.
[49] *L'Andrographe*, p. 195.
[50] *Ibid.*, p. 100.
[51] *Le Thesmographe*, p. 110.
[52] See *Les Nuits de Paris*, Boussel edition, "Accident à un sourd," pp. 35–36.
[53] *Le Thesmographe*, p. 109.
[54] *L'Andrographe*, p. 109.

could go astray, turn to begging out of despair, or feel uncared for in the new regime. Restif was willing to sacrifice a portion of free, individual responsibility for the advantages of safety and security. Just as the father had absolute authority over his sons, the State had power over, and care of, its citizens. Thus intimacy of the cozy, paternal famliy, where all limits were clearly defined and each member's place firmly set, was extended throughout the community.

The political form of utopia was not a topic that Restif spoke about with clarity or discernment. The government remained monarchical, a form well suited to his paternalistic bias, except "obedience will be more certain." [55] "Veneration" was due the royal family as well as everyone in a position of authority. The institutions that Restif elaborated were generally super imposed on the existing political regime.[56] The problem of tyranny was not considered and Restif merely indicated, with a platitude that went back at least to Fénelon in Louis XIV's reign, that "in order to govern justly, one must know the needs and capacities of those governed perfectly. . . ." [57] Leaving the king to his own methods, Restif closed the discussion of political forms.

E. The Prize System and the Nobility

Equality in utopia was also limited by a class system based on ethical merit. In addition to producing a ranking for marriages, the moral register determined the social status of utopians. Restif has been misread as intending to base social rewards on economic merit,[58] as I have already attempted to show, merit was determined primarily by ethical stature and, to a far lesser degree, by "exercizes" or economic accomplishments.[59] A complex system of prizes consisting of differently colored clothing, badges, ribbons, and crowns indicated social rank in utopia. Prizes were awarded according to the Moral Register. An intricate hierarchy of ranks carefully distinguished the behavior of utopians in morals and work. One could rank as a "Tertiaire-Quartaire" respectively in morals and work and thereby receive the prizes of wine-colored clothing, a black cockade, and a pale red crown.[60] Typically, Restif paid obsessive attention to utopian regulations in all their minute complexity. Since social status was

[55] *Ibid.*, p. 192.
[56] See *L'Andrographe*, p. 196; *Le Thesmographe*, pp. 7, 128–129; *Monsieur Nicolas*, Pauvert edition, VI, 247, 251–252, 256.
[57] *L'Andrographe*, p. viii.
[58] Lichtenberger, *op. cit.*, pp. 219–220.
[59] *L'Andrographe*, pp. 40–53.
[60] *Ibid.*, p. 50.

displayed by attire, emulation was easily evoked, reinforcing the picayune gradations of merit. The bizarre system of prizes was seriously intended to make differences more pronounced. This prize system in relation to ethical standards was a form of social utilitarianism, a theory dominant in France in the latter half of the century. Values and norms, in this view, were socially determined and moral behavior consisted not in deciding what one ought to do by individual judgment but merely in following prescribed standards. By adopting social utilitarianism, Restif had no difficulty in transforming ethical ranks into social ranks. The "tertiaire-quartaire" and the other ranks derived from the Moral Register were somehow integrated into a system of social classes which, more than the childish technique of prizes, subverted the claim of equality.

The large role given to this hierarchy of social classes was nowhere more telling than in Restif's treatment of the French hereditary nobility. Unlike most egalitarian utopians,[61] Restif did not anticipate the disappearance of the privileged nobility in his ideal society.[62] Instead, he assigned them the role of leading the army—the project of perpetual peace was chimerical to him.[63] All that he demanded was that they fulfill their soldierly functions. Restif did not earn the approbation of the noble class, however, and as soon as his censor, the philosophe-oriented Pidansat de Mairobert, was replaced by the more rigorous Abbé Terrason, in 1780, Restif bowed to the authorities and softened his attack on the nobility. Chadourne and other commentators have seen in this an obsequious strain in Restif's character.[64] There is little to substantiate this view in his utopian works. Restif was always suspicious of fanatical egalitarianism that would destroy the nobility by force if necessary; he later criticized the Jacobins on this count. Then again, he seemed proud of his treatment of the nobility in the utopias when he printed a letter in Les Contemporaines from his friend Viscount Toustain de Richebourg, which praised his reform for not "imitating the detractors of the nobility. . . ."[65] Also, in Les Gynographes (1777), before the change in censors could restrict his opinions, Restif included the noble classes in his reform.[66] Equality in utopia was thus limited by the existence of a privileged

[61] See Vairesse, History of the Sevarambians (London: Noon, 1738) p. 171, and Morelly, Naufrage des isles flottantes (Paris: Société des libraires, 1753), pp. 1, 18.
[62] L'Andrographe, pp. 85, 123, 181, 182; Le Thesmographe, pp. 133, 136.
[63] Le Thesmographe, p. 133.
[64] Marc Chadourne, Restif de la Bretonne, ou Le Siècle prophétique (Paris: Hachette, 1958), p. 209.
[65] Les Contemporaines, 13, viii in back of book in a letter dated August 25, 1782.
[66] Pp. 85–90.

nobility. The splendor of the parasitic classes appeared, as late as 1782, too much a part of society to be forgotten in utopia.

To the extent that the Cartesian method of doubt had been applied to social authorities by the philosophes, Restif, who carefully reerected social hierarchies, may be viewed as the last voice of the eighteenth century turning against itself. By throwing out traditions and conventions, by stripping the individual of archaic social fetters, the Age of Reason, in Restif's eyes left man naked and grasping. Though he would not restore the authority of the Church and the nobility to its preeminent position in society, neither would he institute the bourgeois ideal of civic and legal equality. The two alternatives in Restif's utopias both rejected a social structure designed for Helvétius' self-interest doctrine. Morality was more than a harmony of selfishness. If men were naturally brothers, the vision of *La Découverte australe par un homme volant* was relevant; if men were naturally fathers and sons, the rigidly hierarchic scheme of the *Idées singulières* was called for. Restif thought man needed both. Both options offered France a community in which men were bound together by emotive as well as rational ties.

VI

The New Morality

The central goal of Restif's utopian writings was the discovery of a new moral principle. He looked for the groundwork of this principle in the nature of man and he developed his new morality by comparing the savage to civilized man and extracting from each type elements that were best suited for his utopia. Thus three images of man lay behind Restif's new morality—savage man, civilized man, and utopian man; this chapter will trace the evolution of his moral principle in each of them. First, however, an estimate of Restif's basic religious stance must be made since it figured in the growth of his moral ideas.

A. Morality and Religion

Only during his youth did Restif accept the Christian dogmas as they were interpreted for him by Jansenist divines. The fierce, unrelenting deity of the Jansenists faded easily before the enlightened doctrines of his friends Gaudet d'Arras, a Cordelier, and Loiseau, a journeyman printer.[1] By the 1760's, the writings of Epicurus and Lucretius had reached provincial Burgundy, and Restif was converted to atheism and materialism. But the blasphemies of the Romans did not hold him for very long. From his earliest utopia in *Le Paysan perverti* to *Le Thesmographe*, Restif provided for a form of worship. During the period of the late 1770's and early 1780's, he vacillated between competing religious postures. Traces of the sentimental deism of Rousseau's Savoyard Vicar always entered into his thinking. "I believe that Religion is a matter of sentiment," he chanted.[2] The trouble was that the spirituality of Christi-

---

[1] *Monsieur Nicolas*, Pauvert edition, VI, 177–184.

[2] *L'Andrographe*, p. 161. See also *Le Thesmographe*, p. 392.

anity had no force [3] and mechanistic Deism appealed to reason, not emotional belief. He quoted an obscure compendium of world religions by Baron de Bernstorf, *Atlas des Religions,* which divided them into two types: those in which the stars were alive and those in which the stars were "machines." [4] Only the former type was acceptable to Restif. He opted for primitive polytheism over Christianity. In polytheism "the Earth Mother" and "the Sun Father" were at least not "strangers"; [5] they could be felt as vital forces in the universe.

Without some form of personal deity, Restif recognized that morality was in danger. "Religion was a bond given to brute man," but it was no longer strong enough to serve as a "solid base for morality." [6] Religion was a "lien" or "fetter" that restrained man's passions, but it had become inefficacious. [7] Notice that Restif was not criticizing religion because it preached false doctrines or led to absurd superstitions. These Voltairean methods of criticism were to him childish and unsuited to the profundity of the question at hand. Restif developed the novel idea that religion was merely another prejudice of man and yet, prejudices were necessary. Against the philosophes who dismissed prejudices as falsehoods beneath contempt for an enlightened man of reason, Restif announced that prejudices could only be judged by the standard of utility. All men had prejudices; some were harmful and some were not. He forecast a work, never completed, which he called *Le Bonheur de l'illusion.* The Catholic practice of celibacy was a disfunctional prejudice because it went against man's sexual needs. The Hindu custom of castes, Restif proclaimed against Diderot, was a useful prejudice because it gave order to society. These judgments were plainly arbitrary. Yet with his revaluation of prejudice Restif approached moral relativism. All customs could be legitimated by their utility; none could be accepted merely because it was traditional. [8]

Restif's projects for religion in utopia had many of the qualities of his cosmogony. Worship would have the character of a primitive ritual in honor of the god of fertility. Dancing, festivity, laughter—these would replace the somber incantations of Catholic masses. [9] In reaction to the morbid Jansenism of his youth Restif proclaimed a joyous religion for

---

[3] *Le Thesmographe,* p. 393.
[4] *Monsieur Nicolas,* Pauvert edition, VI, 151.
[5] *Ibid.,* VI, 134.
[6] *Ibid.,* VI, 60, 148.
[7] *Ibid.,* VI, 201–202.
[8] See *Ibid.,* VI, 78–93, for Restif's discussion of prejudice.
[9] *Le Thesmographe,* p. 120 and *L'Andrographe,* p. 172.

utopia. His "Being Principle"—the only dogma of the new religion—established God as immanent in all creation. The Supreme Being was the essence of nature, pure energy. Although a utopian could feel the presence of this deity, no basis for a principle of obligation was proposed in the new religion. In fact, morality was lifted out of the sphere of religion altogether. Restif's version of ancient Egyptian sun worship did not answer the urgent need for a source of morality.

B. Nature and Savage Man

If religion were not the source of morality, perhaps it could be extracted from nature. In the eighteenth century virtually every theorist announced that his morality was natural. Even the utilitarians, who had rejected the rationalist "natural law" doctrines, tied happiness and utility to nature. In the broadest sense, natural law theorists found nature orderly, rational, and containing a principle of obligation: these attributes were easily deciphered by human reason. Utilitarians, who began with materialist and sensationalist assumptions, viewed nature as the matrix of experience—a laboratory of pleasures and pains. Moral sense theories, particularly the sentimentalism of Rousseau, brought nature closer to a benevolent principle: man was naturally good. Elements of each of these philosophies can be found in Restif's works. Morality was to be sought, first of all, in nature. It had to be fashioned so as to maximize pleasure, which was identical to social utility. The laws of nature were revealed only to the human heart. But Restif did not have the ability to sort out and elaborate a logical ethical philosophy from the general confusion of competing ideas that existed by the end of the century.

To locate Restif's formulation of a natural morality we must turn not to the theoretical arguments of *Monsieur Nicolas*, but to the descriptions of the savage in *Les Gynographes*, *L'Andrographe*, and *Le Thesmographe*. It was primitive man who offered clues about the essential nature of man. Hence Restif gleaned from travel literature "justifications" for his utopian society. His regulations on education, love, work, and social organization were substantiated not by divine revelation or rational principles, but by the evidence of nature as embodied in savage societies. In long sections of the *Idées singulières* Restif described the savages of each continent systematically and with the objective tone of an anthropologist. Like many publicists of the eighteenth century, he was quite familiar with the voyage literature and he was capable of quoting from the most acclaimed sources when necessary: Cook on the South Pacific, Labat and Charlevoix on the West Indies, Smith on Virginia.

Since voyagers had first begun to publish their observations of exotic strange peoples, the savage had presented a moral problem to civilized man. With the image of the primitive, an alternative was posed to the sophistication of European life. Who was better off, happier, and more virtuous, the Polynesian or the Frenchman? The debate over the relative merits of each version of humanity was fundamental to the French utopian thought of the century. It was no accident that More's *Utopia* was presented as the discovery of an explorer. Somewhere, out in a distant sea, might lie an island on which the lost Eden existed.

To the eighteenth-century mind, man was either rude or polished, free or policed, barbarian or civilized, isolated or social, noble or corrupt. The very words captured and held the French imagination. One had to face the problem and take sides, and the side one took determined a great deal about one's ethical position. Savage and civilized man were absolute, mutually exclusive categories and each had its defenders. La Hontan, Raynal, Cook, Bougainville, Labat, Chardin, Charlevoix—ammunition for the debate was plentiful and contradictory. Hume denounced the savage as a vulgar brute; Rousseau celebrated him as noble, moral, and sympathetic toward his fellows.

Behind the bluster of argumentation lay a deep concern: was civilized morality rationally defensible? How were nature and culture to be reconciled? Restif presented the evidence of savage customs to show that morality must begin with an appraisal of the natural essence of man. Civilization was artificial and in need of reform; the reform must be guided by the first principles of human life, unclouded by history and uncomplicated by the arts and sciences. The unusual quality of Restif's descriptions of the savages was just this emphasis on the most primitive customs, the most biologically determined behavior, the human activities that touched the vital pulse of life. South Sea Islanders who murdered their babies, Africans with great erotic needs, Caribs who danced with abandoned sensuality—these embodied savage simplicity. The simplicity of Fénelon's Bétique was quiet, soft, contemplative: Restif's was bloody, throbbing, excited.[10] "The instinct" of the savages "resembles that of animals," he concluded.[11] In short, Restif found the animal beginnings of man in the savage. In savagery he found the prescriptions of nature that justified his utopia and they became the first step in the elaboration of his moral theory.

The conclusions Restif reached about the morality of savages was by

[10] For an example see *L'Andrographe*, p. 306.
[11] *Monsieur Nicolas*, Pauvert edition, V, 189.

no means one-sided. Unlike Rousseau, Restif could not rest with the maxim that nature was wholly good. The savage was as brutish [12] as he was innocent, as treacherous as he was spontaneous, as stupid as he was sympathetic toward his fellow man. The happy Tahitians were contrasted with the ignorant Caribs.[13] Thus Restif unveiled a new explanation for the existence of evil in the world. The facile reasoning of the utilitarians that there was an identity of interests among men, of the moral-sense theorists that man had an emotional propensity toward benevolence, of the Christians that man was born corrupted through the First Fall, of Rousseau that society made men unequal by expanding their *amour propre* were all summarily rejected. Restif proposed that man was naturally evil, that he had as strong a drive to harm his fellow man as he had to aid him. Just as Freud was later to say, this destructive tendency in man was rooted in his biological nature. Here is Restif's formulation.

All individuals love to do evil, to destroy their brothers and other beings. Even herbivorous animals are not innocent; they strike, they bite, they crush. Man loves to destroy for its own sake. I have felt a thousand times the cruel design of murdering a beautiful, large honey bee or drone that came to the pyramidal flowers near my window and I needed to reflect in order to stop myself. What is the cause of this destructive sentiment which is natural to all beings? Is it personal preservation at the expense of other beings? Is it the impulse of nature which, at the same time that it gives life to everything, desires that everything die and gives as many means of destruction as of production? I believe this is so.[14]

Restif believed that nature implanted in man basic drives toward life and toward death, Eros and Thanatos, which only a fool would overlook. Morality had to be constructed on the primitive polar nature of man. In fact the Europeans themselves manifested man's dual ethical nature in their confrontation with the savages. While Rousseau responded to the primitives with openness and warm affection, the colonizers were plundering whole tribes, reducing populations to slavery, raping and murdering helpless natives.

The ancient Greeks, Achilles, Agamemnon, Atreus, Hercules, have they done anything comparable to what the Europeans of the 15th, 16th, 17th and 18th centuries have dared to do? While professing a religion like Christianity, while pretending to embrace the unfortunate Indians, they have enslaved them in

[12] *Le Nouvel Emile*, II, 70.
[13] *L'Andrographe*, p. 253.
[14] *Les Nuits de Paris*, Boussel edition, pp. 76–77.

mines, forced them to plunge into the sea, where they perish by the score, in order to discover pearls. Monsters! Columbus, Pizarro, Cortez, Vespucius, I abhor you all. . . .[15]

Someday, Restif warned, humanity would be revenged for these atrocities.

C. Society and Civilized Man

With the concept of nature determining the essence of man in his raw, animal state, Restif went on to account for the ethical behavior of civilized man. If man's nature was a biological force that pulled in two directions, did civilization fulfill nature? Did it transform natural man into social man by making him moral? Or did it contribute to morality at all?

The word "civilization" appeared sometime after the middle of the eighteenth century [16] and carried two meanings. First, it meant a certain level of rational development. Civilization was tied to a historical process in which faith in progress was germinating. The wonderful prospect of human perfectibility through human reason, the new idea of civilization as a human community guided by scientific advance to ever greater heights of accomplishment—the seed of a belief that Condorcet nurtured in his *Esquisse*—was simply dismissed by Restif. For him civilization had nothing to do with a historical process or the accumulation of scientific knowledge. The whole idea of civilization was undermined by the force of the passions. Happiness related only to the passions, not to the promises of science, and in this respect whether nations were historically advanced or primitive mattered little for the well-being of the people. Man in civilization was no less torn, divided, and two-sided than man in nature. Both were "equally vicious and unhappy." [17]

The second definition of civilization held more appeal for Restif. Civilization did give a different tone to man's conduct. It meant refinement and it gave the passions—tender and destructive, good and evil—an entirely different cast. For Restif, the advancement of the arts and sciences, the enlightenment and refinement of the populace, led merely to a more varied, more intricate manifestation of the same basic passions.

The concept of civilization was best understood in light of the history of language which captured and highlighted the moral quality of human

[15] *L'Andrographe*, pp. 255–256.
[16] N. Hoyt and T. Cassirer, eds., *Encyclopedia* (New York: Library of the Liberal Arts, 1965), p. xxxi.
[17] *Monsieur Nicolas*, Pauvert edition, VI, 128–129.

relationships in a given society. Restif's theory of the history of language was derivative. Lord Monboddo and others had already perceived that language, once the concrete expression of direct experience, had become abstract. Language that formerly embodied reasoning by analogy was now capable of rendering meanings by the use of pure logic. Like Monboddo, Restif reversed the accepted valuation and affirmed the superiority of the language of analogy.

> The simple languages of ancient or modern savages are always analogies to things and only present clear ideas; the languages of policed nations are complicated like Greek and Latin . . . they contain subtle and metaphysical relations, not to things but in terms of an unknown language which is itself complicated. Such is the case with languages formed from dead languages which were already separated from analogies.[18]

"Clear ideas" were not, as Descartes insisted, the result of precise reasoning, but of concrete expression. The symbolic language of mathematics was not the model for all languages, as the English scientists of the seventeenth century had maintained. The romantic temper, reacting to the abstract, overly complex language of the Age of Reason, is evident in this quotation. Restif used his theory of language in practice. His novels, critics maintain, are realistic. *Les Nuits de Paris* portrays the manners of the city in vividly concrete colors. And so, he viewed with dismay a civilization whose language captured only pale reflexions of humanity in its fullness. Civilized language was refined, being more complex and more abstract than primitive language, but this refinement was regrettable because in the process of achieving it the simple, natural experiences of man were lost.

When Restif took a final inventory of the moral products of civilization, he granted it a slight balance over primitive communities. In an important passage in *Monsieur Nicolas*, he tallied the moral score of civilization by making a balance sheet of its advantage and disadvantage. The advantage was politeness, enabling a richer, a more varied existence; the disadvantage was artificiality, or the misplaced repression of the passions. The scorecard looked like this:

> *Advantages:* security, better subsistence, arts and sciences, tenderness, ambition, virtue, the sweetness of friendship, the spectacles, the charm of conversations, "inequality which is an apotheosis of reality for one fourth of the populace," pleasures of "being important, being admired for talent and eloquence, having honor and esteem, being loved and revered," the joys of reading.

[18] *Le Nouvel Emile*, II, 70.

Disadvantages: liberty lost to social superiors, submission to the right of all, subjection to severe penalties, three fourths must be miserable for one fourth to be happy, being exposed to tremble for one's liberty, social diseases like famine and epidemics, fanaticism, the yoke of marriage, *"fetters, which society demands"* and *"which slowly poison life and make it a continual torment"* [emphasis added], taxes, work in the "deadly arts" like mining, "to only exist in and by the opinion of others," "to be led to wars and to massacre or be massacred," to be hanged, quartered, broken, burnt, decapitated.[19]

The great fault of civilization was that it had lost contact with man's biology: it had corrupted nature. Since the customs and institutions of civilization were artificial and bore no relation to man's nature, the equilibrium of the polar passions was disrupted. Restif was vague about precisely how civil society was artificial. He did give some examples; among them he noted that the seasons did not affect life in Paris. Unlike peasants, Parisians lived outside the rhythm of nature. As a consequence of existing outside the natural order of life, the Old Regime was fraught with abuses like wars, taxes, injustice—abuses that were also high on the philosophes' list. The gap in this logic, between the artificiality of civilization and its abuses, was filled by the fetters that Restif mentioned. When he said that civilization created fetters (Rousseau's "chains") he meant that the passionate energy of man was being corrupted. In his vitalist cosmogony, life was energy and the charge that civilization poisoned it was serious. The abuses of the Old Regime were not political injustices; they were abuses against the passions.

In the paragraph immediately succeeding the balance sheet of civilization, Restif spoke of the "necessity of civilization." [20] His judgment was clear. The simple truth was that an alternative to civilization did not exist.[21] The most likely possibility, primitivism, was not viable. With Rousseau, Restif persisted in the belief, contradicted by travel reports, that natural man was isolated and lived alone. Civilization, however, could not be dispersed and its cities abandoned. The sociability of urban society was permanent, but it was not evenly secure. Civilized man remained subject to his passions, passions that could burst forth, dissolving the delicate ties of society in an outbreak of turbulent disorder. Civilization remained a fragile artifice. The danger of violence was great as men in cities could easily solidify into a mob. In *Les Nuits de Paris*, Restif reported over and over again scenes in which the restrictions and inhibitions

[19] *Monsieur Nicolas,* Pauvert edition, VI, 127–129. See *Le Nouvel Emile,* III, 328 for another list.
[20] *Monsieur Nicolas,* Pauvert edition, VI, 129–130.
[21] *Ibid.,* VI, 129.

of civilization evaporated before the savage immediacy of the passions.[22] The mere gathering of a crowd coupled with the intensity of stimulation due to the application of cosmetics and other artifices were a constant threat to civilization. Ironically, civilization had made these phenomena possible in the first place.

Just as the refined condition of man in civilization permitted the growth of cities and their nemesis, the mob, it also worked in a reverse direction by separating man from his fellows. Natural man was isolated and amoral, not relating to other men at all. The morality of civilized man, his conduct toward others, was extremely suspect and at least in need of thorough reform. Fundamental to moral behavior was the "law of reciprocity." Ideally, civilized morality was a disposition to "conciliate our happiness with that of others, and always to subordinate our particular advantage to the common and general advantage."[23] Echoing Rousseau, Restif argued that civilization, through luxury, property, and emulation, did not foster reciprocity but made men egoists, artificially isolating and separating men's mutual interests, and erecting walls that blocked the flow of spontaneous sympathy from man to man. Restif coupled Rousseau's argument with an analysis of the passions in civilization. In their egoistic state, civilized men were unable to express their passions in tenderness, only in Sadean aggressiveness. In his self-contained world, seeking only self-glorification in luxury and other refinements, and without strict, socially sanctioned inhibitions, civilized man could not control himself. Civilized Europeans became "oppressors" of each other and of the rest of the world because of this mixture of freedom and egoism.

Why! Ha! Why has the voracious European troubled the happiness of other peoples, without achieving happiness himself! On the contrary, by exalting his passions, he consumes himself more quickly! One day, one day the peaceful peoples will be revenged! The European will exercise his vile passions on himself; torment himself, oppress himself, starve himself as he starved the unfortunate Hindus! All the harm that he does to others must finally fall back on himself![24]

To the extent that civilization meant refinement it could not be the source of morality.

Restif went beyond the superficial moralism of many eighteenth-

[22] See *Les Nuits de Paris,* Barzun edition, pp. 42, 48–49, 68–69, 132; Boussel edition, p. 63.

[23] *Le Nouvel Emile,* III, 324.

[24] *Les Posthumes,* III, 111–112.

century theorists in his criticism of civilization. He was no fancy gentleman bemoaning the unpolished mores of the new generation. He hit a
note that was sounded again and again in the nineteenth century, culmi-
nating in Freud's *Civilization and Its Discontents*. The target of Restif's
barbs was the structure of civilization itself, not the behavior of a dis-
solute few who failed to live up to a high ethical ideal. His thinking
foreshadows a dissatisfaction with civilization that mounted through the
nineteeneth century. In his biography, Chadourne has called Restif a
prophet because of his uncanny intuition of future lines of thought. The
term is appropriate with respect to his concept of civilization. This extremely eccentric thinker saw that the egotism of bourgeois mentality
effected a drying up of the emotions and that this was an essential feature
of civilization. Restif's cry "O tempora, O mores" had a unique and de-
cidely prophetic ring.

D. UTOPIA AND MORAL MAN

Restif's complaint against the concept of civilization as refinement went
beyond an argument about artificiality. He found the eighteenth-century
notion of civilization at fault in its wanton exclusiveness. When a philosopher like Hume spoke of civilized man, he meant only the higher
ranks of society. To him the unkempt mob that drank gin right out of
muddy puddles in the gutters of London, the foul-breathed mob that
forced polite ladies to hold their noses while riding through sections of
Paris on a festival day, this beast that carried all manner of pestilence and
dirt was certainly not civilized. The critics Freron and La Harpe shuddered with disgust over Restif's novels because his characters and plots,
for the first time in French literature, concerned rude creatures from the
lower depths of the social order. The concept of civilization expressed
in his utopian and moral writings also ran counter to the class assumptions
of his age. Not that Restif prized the workers of Paris or idolized them
as later on the nineteenth century would do—anything but that. Yet his
concept of civilization was democratic in that it resolutely included all
ranks and orders of society. Since the moral civilization would have to
cope with man's passions, omitting certain groups from consideration
would foredoom any plan from the start. All men had passions; all passions had to be purged of their destructiveness; therefore, the moral
civilization had to include all men. We must emphasize this point: in
charting his utopia, Restif always had "le peuple" most immediately in
mind. If his utopia was directed toward any particular group, it was that
of the peasant and the artisan, the day worker and the vagrant, the small

proprietor and the prostitute—in short, anyone who was generally excluded from the thought of most utopians.

Only in utopia could man be truly moral for only in utopia was civilization designed to fit his passions. The return to nature was the return to the biological necessities of the human race. Restif studied man's passions, especially his own, and uncovered the true conditions on which society was based: sexual identity, physical love, hard work, and the different needs of the epigenetic cycle. Only when a society was designed to fit the basic principles of man's nature could civilization become utopia. Total suppression of aggressiveness was possible only by the most severe constriction of desire. Thus Restif developed a new idea of civilization: a social state tailored to suit man's animal nature and, at the same time, sewn together so securely that aggression was hemmed in forever. (Note how close Restif's basic posture was to Freud's, except for the psychoanalyst's faith in individual reason to restrain man where Restif trusted only society.)

This was the core of Restif's utopian vision. It affords an explanation of the unstable balance of his utopian ideal. For although extreme repression was required in order to attain true civilization, it was only available through an unqualified acceptance of the primitive demands of man's nature. Nature and civilization were profoundly at odds, in Restif's view, but they were both necessary for a moral community. In any given work this tenuous equilibrium might be upset and it would appear that utopia wavered toward one or the other pole: either accepting the natural or affirming the social. The reason for the frequent shifts in Restif's position, which we have observed throughout this study, was his own genuine affirmation of the natural part of man—as he saw it. At times he could maintain that free love was possible or that simple equality was the ideal form of social organization because he was deeply attracted by the tender, cooperative side of the passions. A drunkenness with human joys and a sheer delight in pleasure were facets of happiness that he could not completely deny. When he was overcome by the richness and the thickness of sensual pleasure the thought of curbing and renouncing the passions repulsed him. Just such a mood must have inspired the dream of Megapatagonia in *La Découverte australe par un homme volant*. During this rare moment, Restif's fantasy stretched farther than ever before, relaxing the tensions of the eternal struggle between the passions and society. The untroubled tone of Megapatagonia bespeaks a temporary resolution between Restif's warring thoughts.

On the other hand, in the severity of the regulations of *L'Andrographe* Restif emerges as a puritan. Founding a utopia on the true moral principle of reciprocity meant a "continual surmounting of nature in order to do good to others." [25] Essentially, utopia was a land of repression and of an ongoing struggle with the dual nature of the passions. . . . All through the eighteenth century, thinkers tried to find a secular morality that would embody the claims of both nature and civilization. Unanimously, they enshrined happiness as the goal of moral behavior: pleasure was natural since it resulted from the sensual stimulation of man's biological nature and so they called it moral. The weakness of this utilitarian doctrine was that it did not provide a standard by which to judge between two men's notions of happiness that were in competition. Rather, it assumed a harmony of interests, substantiating this by belief in the universal sameness of men. Since reason always led to identical conclusions, all men could agree on what constituted pleasure and happiness. And because the utilitarians rejected natural law theories, they gave up the principle of obligation. Helvétius believed that man did not have to be compelled because he could be conditioned by education.

This easy harmony between nature and culture in the utilitarian ethic was exposed by Restif as a naïve misunderstanding of man's nature. He held that the passions were neither predictable nor tame; they could be destructive and no one's happiness was secure unless everyone's passions were regulated. Restif's principle of obligation was expressed through repressive law. The legislator of utopia established a law for all that was eternally fixed. Restif was unrelenting in his claim that the law must be inviolable and above all men. He saw the sensationalist's dream of inculcating morality by providing proper stimuli as ultimately a hoax. To Restif man was always prey to his passions and the education of these passions was never complete. If Rousseau pleaded for man's natural goodness, man's social goodness was implicit in the thought of the philosophes from Voltaire to Condorcet. It was true that Voltaire spoke in *Candide* of an evil principle in the world, but in general the philosophes were committed to the thesis that man was a manageable creature if only the superstitions and enthusiasms of the priests were eliminated. In contrast to this meliorism of the philosophes, Restif brought back into French thought a principle of evil that was as trenchant and comprehensive as Pascal's. The farcical extreme of utopia's coercive regulations underscored the failure of melioristic thought to account for the fundamental destructiveness of the passions.

The mood of the Enlightenment in Voltaire's *Lettres philosophiques sur les anglaise* and in Diderot's *Supplément au voyage de Bougainville*

---

[25] *Les Nuits de Paris*, Boussel edition, p. 77.

was sharply upset by Restif's utopian vision. Restif gave the word "civilization" a content that pitted it against the strongest arguments of nature: the ability to delay the gratification of the passions. The mentality of Parisians was different from that of the savage in that the former could think in terms of the future while the primitive could act only on the caprice of immediate impulse. Others had given a similar meaning to "civilization" but without stressing the sharpness of its opposition to nature as found in Restif's thought. How could man attain this civilized mentality? Reason was too weak; there was no benevolence or moral sense to inhibit man's actions toward his fellows; no appeal to divine guidance sufficed to defer instinctual needs; feelings of guilt and remorse were too haphazard to offer an effective deterrent. Only society could tyrannize man enough to force him to become civilized. Cultivation of sexual identity, rigid channels for the gratification of love, universal enforcement of work, and the absolute authority of age—these principles of the ideal society reached deep into man's natural constitution and forged it into a civilized mold. The basic ideas behind Restif's utopian vision were intended to constitute a new natural law that could coerce rude nature into the polished refinements of civilization.

PART II
Interpretations of Restif's Vision

VII

Utopia as a Wish-Fulfillment

In the last three chapters Restif's utopian thought will be interpreted as a whole from the perspectives of psychology, sociology, and the utopian tradition. These chapters will attempt to give a pattern to the ideas presented individually up to this point.

Several medical men, mostly Frenchmen, who made psychological studies earlier in this century, label him with awesome diagnostic jargon.[1] He has been called a foot-and-shoe fetisher whose case was complicated by erotomania, mythomania, megalomania, and other related ills. I cannot question these judgments, but it is plain that a definitive psychological study of Restif remains to be achieved. The rich material in *Monsieur Nicolas* offers a strong temptation to the psychological historian. Here I shall attempt only to reach an understanding of Restif's utopias in terms of his own psychological needs. Professor Frank Manuel has indicated the main lines of such an inquiry for a utopian.[2] He views utopias as "private worlds whose geography and laws of movement are explicable in terms of their creator's life experience." Utopia can be ex-

---

[1] Two doctors have undertaken examinations of Restif. The issue between them is fetishism: was Restif a shoe and foot fetisher? Dr. Louis Charpentier in *Restif de la Bretonne: sa perversion fétichiste* (Bordeaux, 1912), and in "Restif de la Bretonne, étude psycho-pathologique," *Hippocrate*, No. 7, Sept., 1934, pp. 577–604, argues the affirmative. Also see an article signed "Dr. Louis," "Un Romancier fétichiste: Restif de la Bretonne," *Chronique Médicale*, année 11, June 1, 1904, pp. 353–357, which is probably by Charpentier. The refutation soon followed: Dr. Louis Barras, *Le Fétichisme: Restif de la Bretonne fut-il fétichiste?* (Paris: Maloine, 1913). Also see the biography by Iwan Bloch, *Rétif de la Bretonne: der Mensch, der Schriftsteller, der Reformator* (Berlin: Harrwitz, 1906).

[2] "Toward a Psychological History of Utopias," *Daedalus*, Spring, 1965, pp. 293–322.

plained on this level as the fulfillment of Restif's deep wishes, as a kind of dream in which unconscious impulses seep into thought,[3] as a compensation for frustrated desires.

A. FROM LOVE TO UTOPIA

Turning to a literary vocation was a crucial decision in Restif's life. His father wanted him to become something more than a laboring peasant, hence the apprenticeship at Auxerre and the life in Paris. Restif did not fulfill his father's expectations after he left La Bretonne. He himself regretted especially his first twelve years in Paris. Working as a journeyman printer by day and becoming embroiled in debauchery at night was a senseless existence. When he became too old to lead the life of a libertine or to satisfy his erotic needs directly, the decision to write loomed larger in his mind. But writing required a capacity for disciplined concentration that Restif had not developed. Finally, in 1767, after false starts and hesitations, his first novel was published. It was a poor product.

The commitment to literature caused a crisis in Restif's life. As a printer he had still been following his father's dictates, since Edme had got him his first job in Auxerre. Now, when he began to write, he was setting off on his own path beyond the security of paternal authority. It was an act of courage for a rude peasant to take up the pen in eighteenth-century Paris, an act almost without precedent. Besides, Restif had little reason for confidence in himself. Already reports on his conduct going back to Sacy showed anything but a praiseworthy record. The imperatives to literature outweighed his doubts, for literature was the only vocation that could bring him relief from the stresses of his inner conflicts. Writing afforded Restif an opportunity to relive his love experiences, and thereby to release his passions, and also to justify his immoral conduct and allay his frightening sense of guilt. Thus he became

---

[3] An attempt has been made by R. Ruyer, *L'Utopie et les utopies* (Paris: Presses universitaires de France, 1950), to paint a profile of the utopian mind. Ruyer's thesis is that there is a basic psychological type of utopian or an "average utopian." (p. 37) Ruyer goes on to give a content to this personality type. The utopian that emerges from his description is an ascetic intellectual who is prone to giving an explanation for the world and also has a tendency toward "the will to power." (pp. 27–40) Ruyer's representative utopian is a theoretical man, a man of knowledge like Plato and More, who also desires to impose his will on the world. Ruyer rejects the following traits in his typology: the economic man, the hero or explorer, the mystic, the man of power, and the artist. This reduction of the utopian to one personality type is not substantiated by any reasonable description of Restif's personality. He was anything but the contemplative scholar or philosopher that Ruyer describes.

a moralist and pornographer, a novelist who portrayed the victory of virtue and the defeat of vice only through powerful and vivid descriptions of the passions.

In *Monsieur Nicolas* there were many indications that writing was a shockingly direct sublimation of Restif's erotic drives; what is more, Restif seems to have been completely aware that his ideas were intimately connected with his sensuality. Here is a remarkable passage showing how he moved from libertinism to the search for amorous satisfaction in the dream of utopia: "Failing the physical satisfaction so ardently desired, my imagination gorged itself on ideas, which at last produced a sort of exhaustion." [4] Like the novels, the utopian writings were part of Restif's system of "muses." His writing was always the result, he claimed, of a direct inspiration from one of his lovers. Only by the stimulation of his passions could he activate his mind for writing. He recalled Mannon Gauthier, one of his friends in Auxerre, and how her sensuality could excite him. "She was dressed with an elegance which roused my most turbulent desires, and as I had no means of satisfying them save by my pen, I hurried to my desk and recorded all the allurements of this mocking damsel." [5] The most prized of Restif's muses was Jeannette Rousseau, a girl he loved with the intensity and purity of Dante's love for Beatrice and Goethe's for Laura. In Restif's tender heart, Jeannette was too celestial to be approached and love's chance was lost. When he later reflected on his missed opportunity he realized that he had lost not only love but intellectual greatness. The powers of this muse would have been unimaginable. "O Jeannette, child of Heaven, if I had seen you every day . . . I should have become as great as Voltaire and left Rousseau far behind! You enlarged my soul: I was no longer myself, but an active, ardent spirit, sharing the genius of the Gods!" [6]

Romantic delusions were mixed here with an acute understanding of the passions and the process of their sublimation. Much of Restif's writing reflects this same blend of emotional effluvia and the touch of genius. It is often impossible to separate the outburst of feeling from the thought intertwined with it. He wrote with passion and his writing reflects an intense state of stimulation barely controlled enough to guide his pen from one statement to the next. Whether due to the "muses" or not, his two hundred volumes read as if they were written during intense emotional states, not in the calm state of contemplation under the steady hand of reason. Restif proclaimed his own condition: "It is not the effect

---

[4] *Monsieur Nicolas*, Ellis edition, I, 359.
[5] *Ibid.*, II, 216.
[6] *Ibid.*, I, 304.

of work nor the fruit of my mind: I have seen, I have felt and I have rendered; feeling alone has guided me. . . ." [7]

Writing was urged on Restif by the intensity of unfulfilled erotic drives that he called his muses. Composed in such emotional states, his books not surprisingly show little trace of careful reworking and it is comprehensible that he composed some of his books directly into the printing press, without so much as a first draft manuscript. His writings were verbalized emotions and they were sacred to him. "Forgive the digression, dear Reader! What would you do? Things come back to me, and involuntarily I write them down; and once written, I would think it a falsification to delete them." [8] The santification of feeling was a psychological need for Restif and was a prime ingredient in his utopias. Writing the utopias and living in the dream world were imaginary jaunts that provided a needed outlet for his passions. Hence to interpret his ideal society as a personal wish-fulfillment is not only justified; it is necessary for a complete understanding of the utopia itself.

B. The Hopes of a Libertine-Moralist

The illumination of Restif's utopia through psychology provides an explanation that runs parallel to the basic theme of the previous chapters. Where his utopian thought manifested an underlying struggle between polar extremes of nature and civilization, at the level of personal dream his utopia reveals a similar tension between the need for release of powerful passions and an opposite need for unbending, all-encompassing controls. Based on the previous chapters, several general themes can be extracted from the *Idées singulières:* (1) the work as a whole forms an intricate architecture of regulations, (2) these regulations are severely repressive, (3) they concern the passions to an extraordinary degree, and (4) their purpose is attainment of happiness by the gratification of the passions. From this outline the conclusion is warranted that Restif had two basic needs which were in polar opposition and which he experienced with equal intensity: the need for erotic gratification which was instinctual and the need to repress and control these impulses which was a demand of the superego. The tension between these needs was sharp and ubiquitous in Restif's ideal world.

From early youth, Restif's temperament and education reinforced each other, intensifying his polar style. In the novel, *La Vie de mon père,* he described in highly idealized and nostalgic tones the traditional patri-

---

[7] *Monsieur Nicolas,* Pauvert edition, VI, 501.

[8] *Monsieur Nicolas,* Ellis edition, III, 115.

archal atmosphere in which he spent his youth and which implanted in him a lofty sense of moral purity and inflexibility. If we can trust his description, Edme, his father, provided the model of steadfast behavior for Restif in which actions were judged by a consciousness of right and wrong, by dictates of the superego. Edme, the story goes, was not a brutal or arbitrary man. His authority was based on his own righteous example and it was imposed by the force of his word, not by beatings and threats. The household of the peasant-patriarch was the epitome of order and harmony; because everyone knew his respective rights and obligations, transgressions of the law of the family were few.[9] Rebellions by Edme's sons were treated as sins disruptive of the natural order of things. Restif never rebelled, at least not outwardly. His own moralism was an obvious replica of his image of his father. His sense that he knew the way things should be—that they should be orderly and that every man had to fulfill his appointed role in the social hierarchy, that laws had to be strict in order to be effective—all such dogmas were superego ideals that he inherited from his father. The parallel of Edme's setting the rules at La Bretonne with Restif's utopian legislation bears witness to the force of the moral commands Restif absorbed during his youth.

The strictness of Edme's moral behavior was seconded by the Jansenist milieu at Sacy. The priest and the schoolmaster maintained a tight discipline among the villagers. These venerable men taught Restif early to avoid sin and misconduct, impressing on the young boy's mind fear of a vengeful God. "It was not men I feared: they knew nothing of my crime; but I saw the God of vengeance, the unrelenting Judge single me out with a gesture awful and horrifying!"[10] During a stay at a nearby village, Vermenton, Restif found that the Jansenism of his host completely disrupted his equanimity. "I nearly fretted myself to death while with Madame Linard, no doubt because of her husband's punctilious disposition. His constant scrutiny, his minute attention to each one of my actions, inhibited me to a point where I could not eat in his presence."[11] Restif's difficulty with the Jansenist church came when he went to Bicêtre, a seminary established in the Parisian hospital, to study under the aegis of his austere half-brother, Abbé Thomas. At Bicêtre Restif found himself in a totally puritanical system. His erotic nature, directly confronted with a Jansenist ambiance, soon burst forth, and when some of his obscene writings were discovered, he was forced to leave the school. Thus came about Restif's ambivalent response to moral authori-

[9] See *La Vie de mon père*, pp. 217–220, for a description of Edme's rule.
[10] *Monsieur Nicolas*, Ellis edition, II, 48.
[11] *Ibid.*, I, 120 *n*.

ties. He was able to maintain a positive identification with his father, but not with other figures of authority in his youth. Possibly his lack of rebelliousness toward his father was only a superficial calm hiding deep-rooted feelings of hostility that showed themselves only in connection with other authoritative persons. His writings, in later years, were marked by his antipathy for Jansenists and all forms of puritanism, but they were equally marked by an unbending sense of moral righteousness.

Restif's erotic needs were also evident even earlier in his youth. Sensual memories reaching back to the age of four [12] were stimulated by licentious stories told by the Courtcou brothers who worked at Le Bretonne. Later, in Auxerre, Restif was instructed in systematic libertinage by Abbé Gaudet d'Arras, a renegade Cordelier who, according to Restif, urged him to seduce Madame Parangon.[13] Even without the influence of the Courtcou brothers and Gaudet d'Arras, however, Restif's sensuality had erupted many times during his youth. The story of these early years, like that of his life in Paris, consisted of a long series of minor infatuations and serious affairs. While he was at Bicêtre Restif foreshadowed his later utopias by writing an obscene poem, the one that got him in trouble, in which he surrounded himself with the twelve girls he desired most in a small hideaway in the mountains near Sacy. A similar theme was used in his unfinished *L'Enclos et les oiseaux*.[14] Thus did Restif's youth manifest the same polar struggle between the id and the superego that was later to be a strong ingredient in his utopias.

Although a stern moral attitude was prominent in Restif's character and utopias, love was for him the most important experience in life. What should one do during the brief wisp of time allotted on earth? Human life is a tale told by an idiot, without meaning except for evanescent moments of sensual happiness.

O happy times, and even now balm to my life! And yet what were you? Passing dreams of an illusory happiness, but so sweet as still to lay charm upon my pain! O happy times! As a wave passes urged by the one behind, always different, always seeming the same, so you passed, and so do all life's moments pass: they fly and are gone forever, yet time seems always the same. The human river of age, maturity, youth and infancy, flows on and we see the same follies and the same crimes, thinly sprinkled with virtues. An immortal watching from afar would think man eternal as himself; yet he exists but for an

[12] See Chap. 2, note 55.

[13] The existence of Gaudet d'Arras has been questioned by Marc Chadourne, *Restif de la Bretonne, ou Le Siècle prophétique* (Paris: Hachette, 1958), pp. 83–96.

[14] See Pierre Louys, "Un Roman inédit de Restif," *Revue des livres anciens,* I (1913), pp. 87–94.

instant! One moment of life, often of misery, and he vanishes forever into the gulf of eternity, as the river is engulfed by the sea! [15]

Restif's response to the passage of time was to commemorate and sanctify love. *Monsieur Nicolas* was a serial of amorous adventures, extending for several thousand pages. From Marguerite, when he was only a boy, to Sara, when he reached the age of forty-five, Restif's biography was a monotonous chain of brunettes and blondes. His choice was to spiritualize his experience into a religion or to join the chant of Ecclesiastes. Restif attempted the former.

In substitution for a calendar of saints, he actually drew up a chart of the year with each day devoted to one or more of his loves. Then too, each of his novels and short stories permitted him to relive his amorous felicity, as most of them have autobigraphical content.[16] More dramatically, Restif inscribed the dates of his affairs on the walls of Ile Saint-Louis.

. . . for some years I have been much inclined to wander on the Ile Saint-Louis; even before I became acquainted with Sara, I had engraved the dates of the principal events of my life on the stones. The following year on the same day, I re-read them; and, carried away by a sort of drunkenness at being still alive, I kissed them, and traced them anew. . . .[17]

In the even march of time, certain days became holidays, sacred interludes in the meaningless flow.[18] The memory of love united the past with the future, making the present bearable—or drowning it completely in an orgy of revivified emotion.

The tour of the island has become delicious for me; all the days are inscribed there on stone, a word, a letter expressing the condition of my soul. Here, three years that are passed . . . I can see four moments in one single instant. The present moment and three preceding years. . . . This simplifies my existence.[19]

There was another mood to Restif's religion of love, a positive side. Love was the glory of life and he was thankful for his great capacity

---

[15] *Monsieur Nicolas*, Ellis edition, III, 186.

[16] The intimate connection between Restif's life and his novels is the thesis, well substantiated, of Porter's *Restif's Novels* (New Haven: Yale University Press, 1966).

[17] *Sara*, trans. by R. C. M. [Mathers?] from *La Dernière avanture d'un homme de quarante-cinq ans* (London: Rodker, 1927), p. 189.

[18] Paul Guilly, *Découverte de l'Ile Saint-Louis* (Paris: Michel, 1953), pp. 165–166.

[19] Quoted from *Mes Inscriptions* in André Desfeuilles, "Le Griffon de l'île Saint-Louis," *Le Vieux Papier*, 1964, fasc. 208, p. 56.

to feel it. In this case, his memory permitted an even greater multiplication of the experiences of love. "I feel pleasure more vividly than most men during the swift moment of its passing; but that moment is by no means always the most delightful: the rapture of it blinds me; whereas alone, after it has passed, I live it over in imagination and savour it." [20] The frantic search for a feeling of existence more secure than the happiness of the sensual moment was not a malaise peculiar to Restif. It was the general mood of a generation that was no longer satisfied with "egoistic hedonism." [21] The quest for happiness hit a note of despair, but Restif found his own antidote. Love properly ritualized and hallowed could blot out the terror of time, and Restif sought love wherever he could find it: in the streets of Paris at night, in bawdy houses, with actresses, and with other men's wives. Eros led him into the darkest alleys of the city and there Restif became a libertine.

Since Restif's adult life did not conform to his father's scrupulously moral pattern, he felt the need to explain the discrepancy to himself. His autobiography, *Monsieur Nicolas*, served the purpose of a confessional. This enormous monument to himself, published originally in nineteen volumes, recounted the disorderly, rakish existence of a libertine in Paris. The full polarity of Restif's nature emerged in the narrative. Written as an apology for his sins, *Monsieur Nicolas* gave Restif still another opportunity to relive his loves, to reexperience his sensual pleasures, to reignite his passions long after he had become unable to gratify them directly.

I have concealed nothing, honest Reader. You know everything I have done; I have not suppressed a single action. Some of them were bad; you have heard and judged. Now I ask you, if after all that you have read, am I what you would call a libertine, a man devoid of morals? As I cannot hear your answer I will put myself in your place and reply as though you were questioning me: "No, no, I am not a libertine." It needs the habit and the love of debauchery to make a libertine; the term cannot be applied to a busy man who, throughout his life, has done the work of two men, one who is carried away by his passions at times, but has always been recalled to duty—by lack of means if reason failed.[22]

Restif's strong need to be moral was satisfied; his libertinage was reprieved by constant devotion to writing and by the inexorable nature of the passions. In *La Dernière avanture d'un homme de quarante-cinq*

[20] *Monsieur Nicolas*, Ellis edition, II, 202.
[21] L. Crocker, *Nature and Culture: Ethical Thought in the French Enlightenment* (Baltimore: Johns Hopkins, 1963), pp. 251–252.
[22] *Monsieur Nicolas*, Ellis edition, V, 250–251.

ans, which was incorporated into *Monsieur Nicolas,* Restif related the pitiful story of his infatuation for a girl twenty years his junior and her brutal destruction of his sense of dignity. That a man past middle age should be captivated by a young innocent and seek sensual pleasure with her was condoned by Restif on account of the strength of the passions.

Reader, you have followed the progress of the most powerful of the passions. You have seen how it was born, how it developed, how it increased even after injuries and the known unworthiness of its beloved object. You have witnessed its paroxysms, its exacerbations, its crisis; you have seen how this volcano seemed to subside; and then, when one expected nothing more, entered into violent eruption! You have seen how wrongs extinguished it gradually, slowly; how it revived at intervals; how it hurled forth the waters of regret and of affection, with the fires of love and of despair; how a last powerful effort seemed to bring about its total extinction! I am a living Book, O my reader! Study me! suffer my prolixity, my calms, my tempests, my asperities! Remember, to encourage yourself in the task, that you are looking at Nature and Truth, divested of all the romantic ornaments of the Lie.[23]

The confessional nature of *Monsieur Nicolas* and, indeed, most of Restif's writings, served to allay his deep sense of guilt. "I have never," he pleaded, "joined in debauches without being punished immediately by remorse." [24] Restif's moralism saved him from a deep feeling of failure. His polar needs for love and for righteousness drove him on in unrelenting tension. Some critics have explained Restif's nocturnal wandering, as reported in *Les Nuits de Paris,* with dubious proofs that he was a police spy.[25] Being a spy, it is argued, he had to snoop around the streets of Paris to obtain information for the government. But a reading of *Les Nuits de Paris* in light of Restif's needs permits a different explanation. Many of the episodes of the book concerned pretty girls. A man in his forties who could no longer attract young ladies, Restif took to the streets to meet them, to speak to them, and to be with them. The attractions of beautiful women were enough to send Restif out of doors. In the incidents he reported he always played the role of the protector of pretty maidens. A girl was threatened by her friends, by a thief, by an unwanted lover. Restif saw it all and saved the girl just in time. Thus the libertine and the moralist were satisfied night after night.

[23] *Sara, op. cit.,* p. 250.
[24] *Monsieur Nicolas,* Ellis edition, IV, 126.
[25] See Léonce Grasilier, *Rétif de la Bretonne inconnu* (Paris: Margraff, 1927). An opposite opinion may be found in Tabarant's biography.

The last resort of the libertine-moralist was to study his passions. *Monsieur Nicolas* was offered to the public as a "natural history," equal to Buffon's, but dealing only with one man's passions. The theme of "revealing the human heart" was equal in grandeur to a description of all natural phenomena and needed nineteen volumes for adequate treatment. Restif's need for purgation was thus transformed into a scientific project. "I have always sworn to sacrifice myself, to expose myself totally, even to shame myself, for the good of my fellows. By my faults, my mistakes, and their causes I would like them to realize what is the proper training to be given to children." [26] Utopia was not merely the preaching of a frustrated moralist; it was the result of the direct experience of the author. Here is something unique in the utopian tradition. Restif used his life as an experiment, the results of which would serve humanity by being the foundation of the ideal society. All the regulations of utopia were designed to fit the results of Restif's observations. The need for satisfying the demands of the superego for moral rectitude became the first impulse toward utopia.

But what was utopian about utopia? How could Restif's interminable struggle between the id and the superego find an ideal solution? When we interpret utopia as a fulfillment of Restif's personal needs, all the regulations, all the renunciations, and all the repressions are seen to serve one purpose: in utopia, Restif could not go astray; in utopia, even Restif, with his indomitable erotic drives, could not lose himself in debauchery. The whole gamut of laws in five thick volumes, often absurd though sometimes perceptive, was a reincarnation of a personal deity who would continually observe, continually guide, and continually reprimand so that the weak, childlike, human soul would never commit a sin and would never succumb to its passions. But the victory of the superego was never complete and utopia was only tolerable because it was consecrated to the gratification of the passions. Happiness, the *summum bonum* of all eighteenth-century French theorists, was the fulfillment of the passions without worrying about sin and guilt because society was so constructed that immorality was impossible.

Psychologically, Restif's utopia was the opposite of the Heavenly City of the philosophes. If they were rebelling as sons, demanding the abolition of authority and limits on personal freedom, Restif conversely called for a more rigorous imposition of regulations on the individual. This difference was based on a divergence in assumptions between them. The philosophes, in their more optimistic mood, at-

---

[26] *Les Nuits de Paris*, Barzun edition, p. 168.

tributed self-direction and control to man through his reason. Restif, who saw only the passions, demanded an external principle of obligation incorporated in society. Perhaps only because of the intellectual success of the philosophes' program was Restif's utopia possible. As their antithesis, Restif's need for salvation caused him to manifest opposite traits. The issue was drawn out in full: was man capable of the ego control the philosophes proffered? The peasant from Burgundy, who knew the ways of the workers intimately, and knew himself even better, said No. For few people fit better than Restif a famous description of Freud's of the dynamics of the psyche: the id was a powerful untamed stallion, likely to buck and gallop off unexpectedly; the sugerego was a man standing on the ground holding the reins. In Restif's case, he would be a large, burly man with a whip who demanded complete obedience from the horse but rarely attained it. The ego was the rider, perched helplessly between the animal's impulses and the superego's strict commands. When Restif claimed his utopia would provide order and tranquility, the underlying tension in his mind gave his utopia a coloration that was entirely different from the utopias of calm felicity that had been dominant in French thought since More.[27]

Each one of the hundreds of regulations in utopia matched a disorder in Restif's personal life. Wherever he placed a limit, wherever he tried to control social relations, we have a sign of an irregularity in his own life. In areas where he felt he fell short of meeting the stringent moral ideals of his Jansenist education and his father's purity he made sure that no transgressions would occur in utopia. Education in utopia sought to impose clear-cut sexual identities; Restif's homosexual practices indicate an ambivalent sense of his own manhood. Love was to be confined to a monogamous family and premarital sex strictly forbidden; Restif's own marriage with Agnès Lebégue was a failure marked by adultery and final separation in 1784. Love was always to be tender; ferocity marked his erotic habits. Work was to be carefully regulated; nothing describes Restif's work habits better than "disorganization." Age was to be respected and made into a principle of hierarchy; could this rule have been his way of discharging the guilt he felt for not meeting the standards of his father? This analysis of the utopian regulations from the perspective of Restif's psychological needs could be applied to the most minute point in his writings. Utopia was a land where the opposite needs of the flesh and the spirit, sexuality and morality were harmonized in society and did not require the effort of the individual.

[27] Manuel, *op. cit.*, p. 301.

C. The Arrival of the Millennium

If utopia fulfilled Restif's polar needs for repression and release, his anticipation of its actualization posed the same duality. His wish to see his utopian regulations effected in France was marked both by joyous expectation and resigned despair. From More down to the nineteenth century, most progenitors of utopias had some ambivalence about the effecting of their dream worlds. Very few sustained the intense, eschatological hope of the nineteenth-century utopian socialists. The Christian humanists of the Old Regime felt the need to hope for their ideal world, but they presented their utopias partly with a tongue-in-cheek attitude, and they wrote out their plans, to a certain degree, as a literary exercise. For example, Morelly felt it necessary to give an excuse for even making public his ideas in the *Code de la nature* (1775). The utopian code was placed after a discussion of existing conditions, accompanied by these comments:

I am giving this outline of laws by way of an appendix and as an excursus, since unfortunately it is only too true that in our day it would be practically impossible to establish such a Republic. . . . I am not so rash as to pretend to reform humankind; but I have courage enough to tell the truth. . . .[28]

These prerevolutionary utopian worlds lacked the total seriousness and sense of urgency of a Saint-Simonian who searched the world for a high priestess to establish the religion of love. Until the close of the eighteenth century, utopians were not absolutely committed to their visions of the ideal society.

Although Restif maintained the divided attitude of his contemporaries, he did so in a way that made him a precursor to the deeply serious utopians of the nineteenth century. On this question there is something of an evolution in his thought. The second volume of *Les Contemporaines*, including "Les 20 épouses des 20 associés," was published in 1780. Here Restif was optimistic; he felt that people might go out and actually set up little associations modeled after the one he outlined. "I have reported this piece of news, honorable reader, with a view to engaging other citizens to imitate this happy association. . . ." [29] In 1781, Restif was less hopeful about *L'Andrographe*. Although he could not expect his reforms to be executed, at least they had a heuristic purpose.[30]

[28] F. and F. Manuel, *French Utopias: An Anthology of Ideal Societies* (New York: Free Press, 1966), p. 102.

[29] *Les Contemporaines*, II, 455.

[30] *L'Andrographe*, p. 201, and see p. 7 of Preface.

The great change in his attitude toward utopia came, as we might expect, with the success of the Revolution in 1789. Dedicated to the Estates General, *Le Thesmographe* was probably one of the first utopias presented as a realizable goal in the present. "Alas! I have never hoped for the happiness of seeing it realized except in these times of regeneration. Ah! If it could be true! what pains could be spared! what a happy confraternity would be immediately established among men! O legislators, I repeat, deign to read *L'Anthropographe* [another name for *L'Andrographe*]." [31] The revolution had stirred tremendous hopes in the breast of the utopian, but when government succeeded government, with a heavy toll in lives at each passage, Restif's dreams grew stale. After 1796, with Thermidor and the Directory, after he had lost a comfortable income by the inflation of the *assignats*, hope seemed foolhardy and the loose tone of life seemed better than regeneration through virtue and terror. Now he exhorted that man could never create a good society and utopians were idle if not dangerous dreamers.

. . . man can never create true happiness, or unhappiness. To establish laws, religions, institutes is only twaddle; he creates nothing and makes only displacements. Inconvenience always accompanies what he adds to nature. . . . Montesquieu and Rousseau were great fools . . . L'Abbé de Saint-Pierre and Chamousset were also fools. As for myself, by publishing *L'Anthropographe* whose execution is now impossible given our morals and our passions, I also was touched by madness, because if men were to execute my plan they would sacrifice more than they would acquire. It is better that they wish to remain as they are. And what of Revolution. Nonsense! Men will only gain the pain that always accompanies change. [32]

Partly due to the revolution and partly as a result of the extremely divergent nature of his hopes, Restif dreamed of his vision with changing emotional hues. The intensity of these emotions at times approached the eschatological sense of salvation of the later utopian socialists. In the early 1780's his attitude toward utopia, with a slightly higher dose of seriousness, was more or less that of Morelly and the quiet ambivalence of the whole Morean tradition. After the Revolution the contradictory nature of his dream of severe repression and fulfillment of the passions became more pronounced. In the excitement of the revolution Restif's attitude swung from one pole to the other; first utopia was imminent, then it was absurd. The delicate psychological balance of the Old Regime,

[31] *Le Thesmographe*, p. 586.
[32] *Monsieur Nicolas*, Pauvert edition, VI, 97; see also VI, 47, 355.

wishing for utopia but not counting too heavily on the perfectibility of humanity, was graphically upset in Restif's mind during the revolutionary years.

D. UTOPIA AND THE AGE FOR RENOUNCING THE PASSIONS

From 1767 to 1802, a period of thirty-five years, Restif published novels. His utopian writings cover almost as long a span of years. But the central period, the time in which his utopian vision crystallized, was the five years that separated *Les Gynographes* (1777) from *L'Andrographe* (1782), including *La Découverte australe par un homme volant* (1781). The late 1770's and early 1780's were in addition his most creative and prolific period in fiction. The first volumes of *Les Contemporaines* appeared in 1780. *La Vie de mon père* was printed in 1779. He began to publish *La Paysanne pervertie* in 1782. During these years his ideas for *Les Nuits de Paris* and *Monsieur Nicolas* were beginning to take shape. Most interesting of all, however, is the fact that the period was marked at beginning and end by two novels that reveal psychological changes in Restif that were crucial to his utopian thought. In 1777, the same year as *Les Gynographes*, *Le Quadragénaire, ou L'Age de renoncer aux passions* was put on sale. In 1783, one year after *L'Andrographe*, *La Dernière avanture d'un homme de quarante-cinq ans* was published.

Both novels relate autobiographical material. *Le Quadragénaire* was inspired by Virginia [33] and was the first novel in which Restif made "considerable use of his life in Paris." [34] The plot of the novel depicted love affairs between a middle-aged man and young women, transparently matching Restif's affairs in *Monsieur Nicolas*. What Porter, from a literary point of view has called a "silly plot," is fraught with meaning with respect to Restif's polar nature. The hero posits that the age of forty (Restif was forty-three) is the time "to take on the respectable quality of a father of a family," [35] in other words, to become a patriarch like his own father and to give up debauchery, "to renounce the passions." Restif could do no such thing. His wife Agnès had left him for the country. There, with her daughters she provided a stable environment for her family by opening a school. It was no accident that Restif considered himself an educator in *Les Gynographes* and *L'Andrographe;* the utopian was in competition with his wife. Although Restif recog-

[33] Porter, *op. cit.*, p. 268.
[34] *Ibid.*
[35] *Ibid.*, p. 270.

nized his parental duties, although he could not escape the severe moral model his father had driven deep into his consciousness, in *Le Quadragénaire* and in his life he cast virtue aside and followed the impulses of his passions by pursuing young virgins. Thus he wrote in *Le Quadragénaire*, "For me, to love is to exist and existence is always worth more than nothingness." [36] The great ambivalence of his life now became manifest when sexual virility began to ebb in middle age; indeed it was exacerbated to heroic proportions: to follow the moral dictates of the superego or to fulfill the passionate demands of the id. The accumulated strains and stresses of Restif's lifelong inner struggle reached their crisis in these years.

By 1783, in *La Dernière avanture*, the situation had taken a new and even more pressing turn. *Le Quadragénaire* questioned the morality of love at middle age; *La Dernière avanture* described with brutal realism how misguided was the quest for love by a man of forty-five. Restif was forty-nine; there can be no doubt of the autobiographical nature of *La Dernière avanture* for Restif included it, only slightly altered, in *Monsieur Nicolas*. Now the hero had become a lecher whose passions had lost their exuberance and vitality. His love was laughable, quixotic, without the redeeming grace of nobility. The man of middle age had wrinkled passions. If he was naïve enough to fall in love he appeared disgusting. The heroine Sara was a coquette who lured him into supporting her and played with his amorous feelings with barbaric frivolity. She two-timed him while keeping his love alive. Restif was not so simple-minded as to blame the girl completely for his own folly; he was aware of the true reasons for his romantic debauchery. They were his own doing. The passions of a man of forty-five were not suited to a love affair with a spirited adolescent. Restif's dilemma was no longer tragic; he no longer had the option of love. The life of a libertine, reaping the only real pleasures of life, was forbidden a man no longer in his prime. The urgency of virtue could no longer be escaped.

In just this tense mental frame Restif wrote his utopias and herein lies their psychological explanation. They were written under the compulsive need to be moral and they demonstrate fully Restif's determination to renounce his passions and vindicate his moral nature publicly. He himself was lost, for the struggle between the libertine and the moralist would continue to the end of his life. But as, with his advanced age, the release of his passions became more and more unacceptable to his Jansenist superego, his need for moral purgation was met by outlining

[36] Quoted in *ibid.*, p. 270.

projects of an ideal society in which others could be saved from his sins. By frankly accepting what he knew to be true, that man in essence was a passionate being, he could construct a utopia in which his own ambivalences would be eliminated and, at the same time, the public would recognize his virtuous intentions. When "the age of renouncing the passions" had come, when the tension within Restif's personality reached a climax, utopia attained its classic expression and was the creative response to a psychological dilemma.

The psychological pattern [37] of the utopian can be drawn in bold lines. Restif was a man—if not of genius, at least of extraordinary nature—whose life was filled with mental tension. When the tension reached its height during middle age, Restif sought resolution for his difficulties by writing utopias in which these tensions were projected onto and overcome for society. The utopian found the key to society's ills while really resolving his own conflicts. To the extent that the individual's conflicts were also those of society, the utopia was an important creative act. If Europe too felt the same conflict between virtue and the passions, between the good and the pleasureful—and judging from the enormous amount of ethical literature produced during the century, it certainly did—Restif gave a utopian image to its solution.

[37] The model for this interpretation may be found in E. Erikson, *Young Man Luther* (New York: Norton, 1962).

VIII

A Sociological Perspective

Can Restif's utopias be interpreted as a reflection of the assumptions of his social class? Do the plans for an ideal society bear witness to the influence of class structure on thought? In this chapter Restif's utopian thought will be explained from the perspective of the sociology of knowledge.

Which social class did Restif represent? Which layer of the social structure fits this Grub Street novelist, this Parisian printer, this Burgundian farm boy? He always identified himself as a peasant. Still, his life took him beyond the barnyard and he lived the sociologically vague pattern of a bohemian. To represent him as a peasant would be an oversimplification. Even if it could be agreed that he was only a peasant, a sociological interpretation of his utopias as an expression of peasant life and interests would be difficult since the historian's knowledge of the peasant mind is limited.

From the sociologist's perspective it would be best not to attempt to analyze his utopia in terms of a class document but to see it as the expression of the conflict between the town and the country.[1] For Restif saw himself not only as a peasant, but as a peasant corrupted by "the dangers of the city." A dialectic of the competing loyalties of the farmer and the city dweller runs throughout Restif's utopias. The deep social division of the Old Regime between the town and the country figures in

[1] Mannheim's brilliant attempt to include utopias in his sociology of knowledge by treating them as determined by the revolutionary social position of the utopian writer does not avail in interpreting Restif's thought. See Karl Mannheim, *Ideology and Utopia* (New York: Harvest, n.d.). Although Restif's utopia broke the bonds of the existing reality, it cannot be said to reflect the wishes of an oppressed social group.

Restif's thought as a parallel to the struggle between the superego and the id. The rude peasant had to transform himself into a refined burgher; the instinctive needs of the passions had to be accommodated to the moral needs of the conscience.[2]

A. A CLASS INTERPRETATION?

1. The Salons

Restif's feelings toward the different social ranks undercut the contention that his utopia was a reflection of the peasantry. His knowledge of the different layers of society varied greatly. Not until after he had written his major utopias, sometime before 1785, did he gain admittance to the salons and begin to learn the ways of the nobility. Only after nine years of publishing novels did he achieve a success: in 1776 Le Paysan perverti was published and soon received public acclaim. By 1782 he had met Mercier, whose praise for Restif was unlimited. Mercier introduced Restif to salon life and they became close friends.

Restif frequented two salons in the 1780's, neither of which was considered first rate among socialites. First, he was invited to the bizarre festivities held twice a week at Grimod de la Reynière's. Grimod was one of those pleasure-loving, decadent aristocrats, men with plenty of money and little to do, who appeared with increasing frequency in the last decades of the eighteenth century.[3] Grimod took great pleasure in giving sumptuous déjeuners philosophiques at which all conventions were broken. A complete sensualist, he spared no expense to delight his literary guests. Emphasis was on the macabre. Initiation to the salon consisted in downing eighteen cups of coffee.[4] Instead of napkins, the guests dried their hands on the hair of the waitresses. The fashion was to publish one's thoughts so Grimod wrote Réflexions philosophiques sur le plaisir par un célibataire (1783) and Almanach des gourmands (1803–1812) in which he systematized his combination of sensual pleasures and philosophical discourse that Restif enjoyed during his visits. The salons at Grimod's became the talk of French society, and here was the place that Restif made his debut. With his strange manners, his worn out cape and his

---

[2] Iwan Bloch, Rétif de la Bretonne: der Mensch, der Schriftsteller, der Reformator (Berlin: Harrwitz, 1906), p. 3.

[3] See G. Desnoiresterres, Grimod de la Reynière et son groupe (Paris: Didier, 1877). At Grimod's Restif met Fontanes, Chénier, Pelletier des Forts, Palissot, and others.

[4] Léon Béclard, Sébastien Mercier, sa vie, sa oeuvre, son temps (Paris: Champion, 1903), p. 720.

repertoire of risque stories, Restif made a great hit at these gatherings. For a time, he was a fad in Parisian circles: every hostess simply had to have *le hibou spectateur* for the amusement of her guests. The man who wrote *Le Paysan perverti*, a book that described such violent passions, had won the hearts of French society. Personages of importance— Talleyrand, Mirabeau, Sieyès, the Duchess of Luynes—flocked to the salon of Sénac de Meilhan to meet this extraordinary man. Restif had become à la mode.[5]

At his second salon, that of Fanny de Beauharnais, Restif met a less outrageous segment of the leaders of France. Fanny de Beauharnais attracted second rank luminaries. At her salon, Restif dined with the poet Dorat, Abbé de Mably, the critic Dussault, the poet Cubières-Palmézeaux, and Mercier.[6]

Attendance at the salons, mingling with men of letters, statesmen, and noblemen, did not alter Restif's opinion of the leaders of France. They were raucous, arbitrary, haughty, and often took cruel advantage of their privileges.[7] But his antagonism against the high and noble ranks could not be termed class consciousness. When the choice was between the aristocratic regime and the Jacobins, he sided with the former because they were less cruel. In a footnote to an episode in *Monsieur Nicolas* which condemned the insolence of the nobility, Restif revised his judgment in light of the events of the revolution.

This was written in 1784, I would not say the same thing today, the 15th of August of 1790, and today the 18th of March 1795, I would add a remark on the cruelty of the Jacobins. What then is the conclusion? That all tyranny is intolerable, and the tyranny of the *sans-culottes* even more so than that of princes. For princes do not oppress everyone, because they do not know everyone; whereas the innumerable tyrants of the *sans-culottes* are everywhere. They are malicious, jealous of their equals, drunk with the power to oppress.[8]

This much can be said: utopia was not the dream of the peasant-worker against the upper classes; it was not a revolutionary document arising from the history of class warfare. Restif resented the arbitrary domination of the hereditary nobility, but he was not possessed by the idea and he did not make it a guideline of his ideal society.

[5] *Ibid.*, p. 730.

[6] A. Naughton, *Le Tableau des moeurs dans les romans de Rétif de la Bretonne* (Paris: Presses modernes, 1929), pp. 41–42.

[7] *Le Palais Royal*, p. 151; *Monsieur Nicolas*, Ellis edition, IV, 246; *Monsieur Nicolas*, Pauvert edition, VI, 122.

[8] *Monsieur Nicolas*, Ellis edition, IV, 246.

2. The Streets

From 1751 to 1767, first in Auxerre and then in Paris, Restif worked in the printing trade and had ample time to learn the manners and complaints of the workingman. When he arrived in Paris he got a job at the Imprimerie Royale and experienced exploitation first hand. From a total salary of one hundred *sous* per week, he received only fifty because the Director took the other half for himself. There was nothing to be said and no one to appeal to.[9] Restif also spent most of his time with the lower classes and most of his friends were *routiers*. The constant complaint from La Harpe about Restif's novels was that they spoke of vulgar subjects, drawn from the streets, and had no interest for a man of letters.[10] Restif defended his choice of subjects: the people were the majority and one had to learn about them.

. . . I must dare to say it: that I am perhaps the only man, and surely the only writer, who sees things in their true perspective. Once all our witty authors, our elegant artists are hurled into fashionable society, they see nothing else. I alone, the day after dinner with a duke and a peer, supper with a pretty marquise, a witty and talented countess, return to ordinary clothes and heavy shoes, in the midst of workers of the most common sort; not playing the dandy or the fine gentleman with exaggeratedly elegant manners, but working with them, like them, reading the depths of their souls and consequently seeing cause and effect [of the events of the revolution].[11]

In this paragraph Restif demonstrated a new point of view: real life, the true social reality, was to be found not among the nobles but in the bosom of the populace. *Les Nuits de Paris*, the result of his meanderings and observations of the people, was a new form of literature, a kind of journalism about daily life. Mercier's similar work, and its only competitor, *Tableau de la vie*, lacks the vivid descriptions of *Les Nuits de Paris*. Restif's interest was in the life of the common man, an interest that he carried into the making of his utopias where his focus was clearly on *le peuple*. Amidst the aristocratic prejudices of the Old Regime, he insisted that "the people" was a topic of great importance.

Although he ushered in the modern view of the social significance of the people, he did not idealize them as the nineteenth century was to do.

We must admit that in all countries that which is called the people is a ferocious beast! I am a peasant. My attitude toward the people and the nobles is

[9] *Ibid.*, IV, 67.
[10] J. R. Childs, *Restif de la Bretonne* (Paris: Briffaut, 1949), pp. 20, 21, 29.
[11] *Les Nuits de Paris*, Barzun edition, pp. 89–90; see also p. 68.

known. But if I must tell here, without irony, what I think, I must say that all our humanists do not know what they are talking about. For some time the workers of the capital have become intractable because they have read, in our books, a truth too powerful for them: that the worker is a valuable man. Since they have read this truth they have taken it upon themselves to prove it a lie by neglecting their work and by reducing its value at least by half.[12]

Restif did not view the people with the glorified praise of a Michelet. Though he depicted their labors and their joys with concrete, realistic touches, he did not make their case a *cause célèbre*. Utopia was not an ideal society for the working classes, although it was limited by their needs. Restif had specific complaints about the workingman that cannot be attributed to aristocratic insolence but perhaps to a Jansenist obsession with industriousness: they were "gross," [13] at every turn they became "hooligans, thieves, pickpockets and libertines," [14] they lacked discipline at work and loved idleness,[15] and above all, they had turbulent, uncontrollable passions which, when aroused, caused disorder and havoc.[16] It was the passions of the people, in their most hideous display, that Restif made the theme of his writings on the revolution in *Les Nuits de Paris*. To a degree, Restif's fear of the disorder of the people only manifests his inability to adjust to the chaos of metropolitan Paris; it is equally true that his perception of the behavior of the people during the revolution represents to the historian a side of the revolution that is little known about and even then only through the hazy spectacles of the terrorized nobiliy.

3. The Revolution

When the revolution came Restif had already published six volumes of *Les Nuits de Paris*. He continued his nightly sojourns in the streets of Paris during the revolution and Volume VIII of *Les Nuits de Paris* was the product of his commentaries on what he saw, heard, and read about. Volume VIII, entitled "The Revolutionary Nights," has been considered by Taine [17] an important document in the social history of the revolution, and has been translated into English and German. One scholar has awarded Restif the title of "the first of the great sociologists of our con-

---

[12] *Mes Inscriptions*, p. 130.
[13] *Monsieur Nicolas*, Pauvert edition, VI, 87–88.
[14] *Les Nuits de Paris*, Barzun edition, pp. 48–49.
[15] *Ibid.*, p. 132.
[16] *Monsieur Nicolas*, Ellis edition, I, 184.
[17] Quoted in Maurice Blanchot, "Un Livre vivant," *Critique*, année III, No. 4 (March, 1948), p. 197.

temporary era" on the strength of this volume.[18] Restif's interpretation of the events of the revolution was completely in line with his thinking in *Les Gynographes* and *L'Andrographe* and it confirms the thesis that his utopia was not a class document even though it was written with a notion of the people in mind. In *Le Thesmographe* (1790) he still recommended *L'Andrographe* as the best expression of his utopian thought. The judgments he had made before the revolution he continued to take as his final statement.

Restif's publications during the revolution reveal only a naïve understanding of the events he witnessed; he was not an astute political observer.[19] The issues of the revolution, the struggle for power and the triumph of the Third Estate against their social superiors, passed before him without enlisting his notice or interest. His first response to the events was an affirmation of the overthrow of the Old Regime by proposing anew his reforms for society. *Le Thesmographe* and an anonymous pamphlet, *Le Plus fort des pamphlets*,[20] in which the *Idées singulières* was summarized, presented his advice to Frenchmen now that a general restructuring of society seemed imminent. Politically, he suggested that new estates be established to represent the special needs of peasants and women, a continuation of the Medieval notion of right as particular privilege.[21] The other reforms all bore the stamp of *L'Andrographe*: the elimination of a celibate priesthood,[22] the legalization of divorce,[23] the praise for paternal government[24] and, for the economy, the stress on agriculture over commerce.[25] Advertising his own ideas was the extent of Restif's involvement in the politics of the revolution.

[18] Jacques Pinset, "Les Origines instinctives de la revolution française," *Revue d'historie économique et sociale*, XXXIX (1961), p. 228.

[19] *Monsieur Nicolas*, Pauvert edition, VI, 260–309, 325–351 for Restif's treatment of the revolution in *Ma Politique*.

[20] *Le Plus fort des pamphlets: L'Ordre des paysans au etats generaux* (1789) was attributed to Restif by Lacroix, but surprisingly was not mentioned by Childs. There are two substantial reasons for claiming Restif's authorship. First, the reforms suggested in the pamphlet are precisely those of *Le Thesmographe*. It even indicates the author's hatred of lawyers so prevalent in *Le Thesmographe*. Second, "L'Antropographe" is mentioned on page. 8. This was a variant of Restif's other name for *L'Andrographe*: "L'Anthropographe." Dropping the "h" was a spelling Restif often used because it conformed with the reform of *Le Glossographe* by making spelling phonetic. There is little doubt in my mind that *Les Plus fort des pamphlets* came from Restif's pen.

[21] *Le Thesmographe*, p. 7; *Le Plus fort des pamphlets*, pp. 10, 13.

[22] *Le Plus fort des pamphlets*, pp. 54–55.

[23] *Ibid.*

[24] *Ibid.*, pp. 6–8.

[25] *Ibid.*, p. 26.

In fact, his remarks on the events of the upheaval in *Les Nuits de Paris* and in his later works merely express the themes of his utopia. There was but one possible cause for the disorders of a revolution and that was the unleashing of the passions of the people.[26] On November 9, 1788, the printing of the first six volumes of *Les Nuits de Paris* was completed and in them Restif predicted the revolution:

And you, statesmen, beware! A fateful revolution is approaching! The spirit of defiance is spreading, growing! It festers silently in the lowest class! I declare this to you publicly, and if you deign to investigate, you will be shown over-whelming evidence! [27]

A chain of events was in process that had to lead to a revolution: workers received higher wages; they had more free time; idleness led to disorder, disorder to insubordination, insubordination—by cutting the inhibiting bonds of social relations—to an eruption of the passions. The logic was ineluctible.

Even the wives of workers themselves know that the insane increase in salaries is wrong, that it turns coarse men's heads! O Statesmen! I have proof that such a degree of good living, of comfort, cannot be absorbed by people in the cities, though those in the countryside make the adjustment.[28]

The dissolution of social restraints among the workers certainly fails to explain the great events of 1789, but it is a realm of reality that has generally not been illuminated by those who explain the causes of the revolution.

The revolution that Restif described, at times vividly and at times dis-gustingly, was an atrocity and it was committed by revolutionaries who shouted, he wrote, "Long live death." [29] To read his first-hand reports of the nights of the revolution is to read about murder, thievery, rape, and guillotining with crowds rejoicing as they would at a circus. The aspect of the revolution that captured Restif's eye was the cruelty of uninhibited passions. This is not to say that he did not notice the grand events that would transform society: "Yes, whatever happens the lords, the noble-men, the aristocrats of every level are forever lost, not in France alone,

[26] Pinset, *op. cit.*, pp. 198–228 gives a similar interpretation. For a divergent view, see A. Ioannisiani, "L'Utopie de Restif de la Bretonne et le communism utopique," *La Pensée* (March–April, 1958).

[27] *Les Nuits de Paris*, Barzun edition, pp. 68–69.

[28] *Ibid.*

[29] *Ibid.*, p. 300.

but in all Europe—if not during the eighteenth century, then during the nineteenth. The shock has been imparted: a new order of things will begin. . . ." [30] But to Restif the central fact of the revolution was not the change in political regimes or social structure: it was the tremendous loss of life through the eruption of the passions. The "absurd destruction," he sadly and conservatively moaned, was not worth the change.[31] He would settle for the imperfect freedom of the Old Regime. On July 12, 1789, well before other Europeans were horrified by the violence of the revolution, Restif thought the passions had already too much freedom.

And I—I shuddered. I saw a cloud of misfortune gathering over this luckless capital, once the most voluptuous city in the universe, the freest, the most pleasant, and consequently the happiest. . . . For twenty-five years I have lived in Paris freer than air! Two principles sufficed to make any man as free as I am: to be honest, and not to write any pamphlets against the government. Everything else was permitted, and never was my freedom hampered.[32]

As Restif saw it the revolution had nothing to do with wiping away feudal restrictions or the enactment of new laws to reorder society; it was a spontaneous occurrence, sweeping through the lower classes like a tidal wave and causing the social flood of anarchy. The stampede of the masses in 1789 at the Bastille and at the massacres of September 1792 was the picture Restif had of the revolution. During early September 1792 he records this:

There was a pause in the slaughter. . . . Then a woman appeared, white as a sheet, supported by a doorkeeper. Brusquely she was told: "Shout '*Vive la nation!*' "

"No! No!" she said. She was forced up onto a pile of corpses. One of the killers seized the doorkeeper and pulled him away. "Please," the pitiful woman cried, "don't hurt him!" She was told again to shout "*Vive la nation!*" She refused with disdain. With that, a killer grabbed her, tore off her dress and slit her belly open. She fell, and was finished off by the others. Never in my life had I imagined such atrocity. I wanted to run away but my legs failed. I fainted. When I came to, I saw the blood-soaked head. I was told that they had washed it, curled it, mounted it on the point of a pike and paraded it under the Temple prison windows.[33]

In attempting to establish Restif's attitude toward the revolution, scholars have noted strange inconsistencies in *Les Nuits de Paris*. The

[30] *Ibid.*, p. 279.
[31] *Monsieur Nicolas*, Pauvert edition, VI, 391.
[32] *Les Nuits de Paris*, Barzun edition, p. 233.
[33] *Ibid.*, p. 303.

conclusion to the work, entitled *Profession de foi politique de l'auteur*,[34] in particular has been regarded as a statement giving moderate support to the revolution. A degree of ambivalence definitely pervaded Restif's writings on this subject. The revolution had promised much that he had always hoped for,[35] but its performance fell short of its goals and there was the violence to be considered as well.[36] He too had hoped for a general transformation of society, but the dream was lost in the blood of the events.

At the inception of each new government he had to revise his judgment. Before Louis XVI was guillotined, he had hopes for the success of the revolution. After 1792, as the Girondins gave way to the Jacobins, the Jacobins to the Mountain, the Mountain to Marat, and Marat to Robespierre, Restif retreated further and further from the views of his countrymen. The times were dangerous in 1793 and 1794 and in *Les Nuits de Paris* Restif adopted an unheroic posture of discretion, hiding his feelings behind a vague rhetoric of approval for the revolutionary governments. During the rule of the Directory his revulsion for the "puritans," for the "fanatic" Jacobins, and especially for "the infamous Robespierre" came out.[37] If read carefully, *Les Nuits de Paris* and other works published between 1789 and 1794 do not indicate, as some scholars have claimed, that Restif held no position toward the events and merely shifted his views with the corresponding changes in the politics of the governments. Throughout the entire period of stress, his concern for subordination and for order and his fear of the uncontrolled passions are evident. His "profession of political faith" was published sometime in 1794 after the execution of Robespierre.[38] It began with an affirmation of orthodoxy: the Jacobins were "the true national representatives" and Marat and Robespierre were "traitors." [39] He continued with justifications for the death of Louis XVI, Marie Antoinette, twenty-two deputies of the Revolutionary Tribunal and other counterrevolutionaries. Yet the reader must have reservations about Restif's loyalty to the ideology of the revolution. Nowhere in these pages did he applaud its general purpose or results. His profession sounds forced and he wrote only what he had to in order to maintain political safety. Then too the deaths were always approved only as regrettable necessities. He reminded

---

[34] *Les Nuits de Paris*, Boussel edition, pp. 354–359.
[35] *Monsieur Nicolas*, Pauvert edition, VI, 304–305.
[36] *Ibid.*, VI, 307, 352–353.
[37] *Monsieur Nicolas*, Ellis edition, IV, 131 *n*
[38] Childs, *op. cit.*, pp. 303–304.
[39] *Les Nuits de Paris*, Boussel edition, p. 354.

his reader of human frailty and of the need for compassion. Pointedly, he opposed the idea of sin against the revolution by one of his favorite quotes: *Nil humani a me alientum.*[40] His meaning is clear. Forgiveness, not death, should be the portion for political crimes. Nothing human can be so separate or foreign from us that we can remove it by execution. Had the severe legislator of *L'Andrographe* mellowed?

For political crimes Restif suggested leniency, but the core of the revolution—the unleashed passions—had little to do with politics. By not treating the role of the passions in his apology Restif could temporize; and that is just what he did. Hence his idea of the origins and aims of the revolution are not amenable to a class interpretation: he abhorred the fanaticism of the middle class Jacobins; he was petrified by the rampaging people; he did not align himself with the counterrevolutionary aristocrats.

B. Peasant and Urbanite

Restif's father was one of the many prerevolutionary peasants who owned his own farm, and La Bretonne was large enough to satisfy the needs of all the Restifs. It must have been fairly large since there were a dozen children to care for. Edme was efficient and self-reliant and these qualities were reflected in the prosperity of La Bretonne. He was a forward-looking man who adopted new techniques and led the village in experimenting with innovations in agricultural science. Annoying feudal restrictions had long disappeared from Sacy and the Restifs lived in security. La Bretonne prospered through the initiative and hard work of its respected master. The villagers of Sacy looked to Edme for more than technical advice; he was revered by them as a just and honest man and he was given a quasi-official judicial post. As the administrator for the lands of three lords, he adjudicated disputes among peasants of the surrounding villages.[41]

Edme appears in Restif's biography, *La Vie de mon père*, as a rural Solomon, whose wisdom and morality were revered by all who knew him. The peasants, who governed their own community through a form of primitive democracy, elected him president of their assembly.[42] Under Edme's aegis, Restif enjoyed economic security and political freedom in his youth. There were no incidents of starvation, no injustices of an arbitrary aristocracy to alienate him from French society. He

---

[40] *Ibid.*, p. 356.
[41] Naughton, *op. cit.*, p. 82.
[42] *La Vie de mon père*, p. 200.

could take pride in and enjoy the emotional security of the patriarchal household.

Restif left this rural arcadia for Auxerre and later for Paris because his father, recognizing his good mind, decided he should not work on the farm but aspire to higher goals in the city. He saw his father's decision as the turning point of his life. Like his fictional characters in *Le Paysan perverti*, he felt that he was corrupted by the city.

I wept for my lost innocence and tranquil life. . . . From the poisoned cup of the towns I have absorbed desires for slim waists, tiny feet and enchanting breasts; for the provocative face, the small voluptuously tilted nose and teasing smile; for pretty childish ways, seductive words, extravagant adornments and lascivious walking; for a deceptive facility and the degrading perfidy of prostitution. O, love of forests, I lost you when I lost my innocence! [43]

The prodigal son complained about the New Babylon. He saw himself as a rude but innocent savage who was not fit for the evil refinements of civilization. He confronted the problem of becoming civilized, of leaping through history in his own life and transforming his primtive nature into the cast of advanced civilization, after he had already attained maturity.

. . . had I known how to go to America, I should have flown thither—not in search of a fortune, but to live as a savage. This was the only manner of life which would have satisfied me; in me nature had to be forced to the mould of civilization.[44]

Restif was quite perceptive about his own difficulties. The town dweller had to be able to control himself, in order to live morally and avoid debauchery, far more than the provincial. Yet more than on the farm, the town dweller had certain freedoms and if he were able to repress his passions, city life offered a wider scope of experience that could be enjoyed without any danger of disorder. At La Bretonne, the limits were set by the community and imposed by the head of each family.[45] The groundwork for utopia was set at Sacy for Restif: society must control the individual and be above him.

However, Restif's own story of the peasant corrupted by the town was not this simple. It was not the one-dimensional tale of a child who was lost in the city and wrote a utopia to regain parental approval. Restif's tale includes the grander theme of the passions. It was human

[43] *Monsieur Nicolas*, Ellis edition, I, 245.
[44] *Ibid.*, I, 242.
[45] *La Vie de mon père*, p. 63.

nature that was at stake: was the city the best environment for the full expression of man's passionate needs? Was the social freedom and individual repression of the city the optimal condition for the primitive savagery of the human passions?

The idealization of the innocent peasant in *La Vie de mon père* and *Le Paysan perverti* did not render the complete reality of Restif's situation. The novelist's tumultuous passions had erupted and brought him disgrace long before the lures of Paris affected him. As has been noted, the Courtcou brothers, Gaudet d'Arras, and the rural girls had provided enough stimulation to arouse Restif's volatile desires. Even the close scrutiny of village authorities did not inhibit him from begetting a child at the age of twelve by a peasant girl. In short, the conflict between town and country was not altogether one-sided and Restif hesitated to assert that the passions were purest in the village. He put the question of their relative merits before himself many times and normally decided in favor of the sophistication and refinement of Paris. One of the major themes of Restif's life and work was this conflict between nature and civilization, country and town. Indeed, the sociological historian might well interpret his utopia in these terms.

A young country boy came to the city, was instructed there, was taught politeness there and became a savant. But ambition and exalted passions caused him trouble; he regretted the tranquility of his first environment. You ask him, would he wish to give up his lights? If he is sincere he will reject this proposition with horror. How many times have I posed this question to myself, in certain very unhappy circumstances: would I like still to be a peasant? At first, at an age when experience had not enlightened me enough, I believed that I sincerely would desire my early tranquility. I left for my province . . . I returned to simple men. But I was only there for eight days when I found them unbearable: their deference, my superiority, the solitude . . . I returned to Paris. Upon seeing this great city, where I have suffered so much, my heart leaped with joy. I blessed it; I swore never to leave it again.[46]

Having decided to remain in Paris, Restif spent his mature life there, leaving it only for short trips back to Burgundy. His commitment—to become civilized, to devote himself to the arts and sciences, and to reside in Paris—was easier to assert than to sustain with comfort. His life in Paris was not at all tranquil; his existence there was a constant battle with poverty and an unending struggle between tumultuous love affairs and equally tumultuous periods of literary activity. To his last days he remained ambivalent about the city. "Paris! at once a place of delights and horrors! at once a filthy abyss where whole generations are

[46] *L'Andrographe*, pp. 183–184.

engulfed and an august temple of Saint Humanity!" [47] In the same un-
certain vein he summed up his four years at Auxerre as a time when he
had been "so happy and so unhappy. . . ." [48] Thus, to anyone who
wished to study man, to see him as the passionate being he really is, Restif
offered this ambivalent advice:

To live always in the country is the means of only knowing one-half of man.
The city shows social man in his highest degree of perfectibility. It is there
that one can see the conflict of all the passions, there that man appears as an
artificial being separated from nature. . . . [49]

In the artificial, civilized environment of the towns, where neither seasons nor climate itself were taken into account,[50] man was "immune"
from nature. And therefore his own nature, his passions, became more
turbulent and uncontrollable. Couple this artificiality with the heightened
stimulation of civilized apparel and the lack of social controls, and you
have what Restif saw as the true dangers of the city. These dangers
caused him to dissipate his first twelve years in Paris. From 1755 to 1767
he worked "like a machine" in various printing establishments,[51] fearing
to assert his individuality, to find his identity and become the man of
letters he was capable of becoming. The peasant was also overcome by
his sensuality and was prey to the perfidious women of the city, like
Henriette Kircher who lured him into marriage and then robbed him
of all his meagre possessions. Until he became alert to Parisian treachery,
the rustic peasant was open to the hucksters and dandies of the big city.

Later on, when its excitement no longer caused so much disorder in
his breast, Restif was able to show very concretely how the city
threatened morality. It transformed people's simplest, most unpretentious
habits into dangerous opportunities for vice.

There is a practice in Paris whereby the capital resembles the provincial
cities . . . in late July, in August, and into September the women sit outside
their doors in order to get a breath of fresh air and chatter among themselves.
. . . In an enormous city, this practice gives rise to various incidents. Lovers
and sneak thieves both have taken advantage of it: the former to make off
nimbly with a woman's shoe and turn it into an object of worship; the latter to
steal a pendant earring, a cross on a velvet ribbon around the neck, or even a
slipper, for the sake of the buckle. The thieves have been known to feign a

[47] *Les Contemporaines*, II, 389.
[48] *Monsieur Nicolas*, Ellis edition, IV, 31.
[49] *Le Nouvel Emile*, IV, 1.
[50] *La Vie de mon père*, p. 212.
[51] *Monsieur Nicolas*, Ellis edition, IV, 68–70.

brawl among themselves, tumble into a group of seated women, and rob them. Love may play a parlor game, and with eyes blindfolded, head pressed between the knees of some fair lady, arrange a tryst under Argus' very nose.[52]

Even a head with one thousand eyes could not prevent an innocent custom of sitting on the stoop from turning into a vicious scene of debauchery and robbery in the streets of Paris.

Restif never managed to obliterate completely his peasant background and live at ease in Paris. For him the enticements of the city always betokened the dangers of disorder, of loss of control. To escape Paris without actually leaving it, to find limits to the city's chaotic anarchy, Restif turned to the Ile Saint-Louis as a plant turns to light. There he found a friendly environment where the walls, standing as limits to hold him back, provided welcome relief from the chaos outside. The island was finite and its restrictions gave Restif the freedom of tranquility. Each night he walked about the tiny enclave as secure as if he were at home, Mercier's description of the Ile Saint-Louis in *Tableau de la vie* suggests why Restif found the island so accommodating.

The Ile Saint-Louis seems to have escaped the general corrupting of manners. No prostitute can find a lodging there; as soon as her way of life becomes known, out she must go. Here the middle class is its own police; every man's way of living is an open book; as for the women, no girl guilty of an indiscretion (and these things are always found out) need ever hope to find a husband in that quarter. This neighborhood is the nearest thing to a third-rate provincial town that Paris can show.[53]

It was the freedom of the towns, just as it was psychologically his own id, that Restif wished to control in utopia. His comments on the revolution reveal that he feared the passions and not any particular social class. His idealization of rural life in his novels had its counterpart in utopia. The tranquility of the passions in Sacy would be surpassed by a calmer and even more secure felicity in utopia. Paris had shown him how far away from nature's roots man could stray. The perfumes and the periwigs, the carriages and the muddy streets, the mobs and the thieves were all vices of the city that stemmed from its artificiality. But the artificiality was enticing and he remained in Paris. Only in utopia did he return to the village where nature's rhythms determined the social order. Yet, even in utopia he could not wholeheartedly recreate the tranquility of rural

[52] *Les Nuits de Paris*, Barzun edition, pp. 65–66.
[53] Sébastien Mercier, *The Waiting City*, trans. by H. Simpson (Philadelphia: Lippincott, 1933), p. 130.

conditions. The natural orders of sexual identity, the hierarchy of age, the biological values of love and work—all these could not be reduced to rural proportions. The sophistication of the city had shown him a multitude of gratifications for man's passions; he could not relinquish them all. Cosmetics and spectacles, symbolically the most artificial of urban inventions, would have to be included in utopia. He would include them by carefully controlling them, by redirecting their use from the corrupt ways of the city, to the virtuous ways of nature. Restif's utopia was not only the waking fantasy of a corrupted peasant in search for his lost innocence; it was equally the dream of a cosmopolitan man of letters, eccentric and at times vulgar but nonetheless a man who had been titillated for fifty years by the city's lures.

IX

Restif and the Utopian Tradition

From the foregoing analysis and interpretation of Restif's utopian thought, his place in the utopian tradition can now be estimated. Beginning with More in the early sixteenth century, and continuing on through Teilhard de Chardin in the twentieth, the European intellectual tradition has generated a long succession of utopians. Restif's significance or lack of significance must ultimately be appraised in terms of the evolution of this mode of thought.

A. Utopia Established and Legitimated

The establishment and legitimation of the ideal society are serious problems in the history of utopian thought. Restif's techniques for the foundation of his utopia were not novel. Like More, he anticipated that King Utopus would read his books and enact them just as he imagined Joseph II had done with *Le Pornographe*. He was not so naïve as to believe that a mere statutory change could bring about the perfect community. The first generation of utopians would not approximate the ideal and would have to be transformed. The importance of the first generation to Restif is evident in the stress he placed on education. That is why the speakers in the *Idées singulières* direct themselves to children. Restif did not envision the transformation of society into utopia as a single violent and disruptive event. He realized that the older generation, and anyone with a deep interest in the status quo, would not easily be converted to his plan. Noblemen, for example, would be extremely hostile to it. When he contemplated strong resistance of this kind Restif, did not advocate dealing with it by coercion but suggested rather that noblemen would voluntarily join utopia as they came to see its obvious benefits. Utopia would not be inaugurated by revolution. In his avoidance of social cataclysm Restif remained in the eighteenth century intellectual tradition. In fact, the violence of the revolution made him seriously reconsider the wisdom of all radical social change.

Another difficulty presented itself: how were the new utopian laws to be graced with moral force? They were drawn up by mortals and thus carried no more weight than competing systems. Why should utopians remain convinced of the perfection of their laws and accommodate themselves to them, renouncing all desire to alter them? Restif's responses to the problem of legitimating the utopian statutes were already thread-bare platitudes to a reader in the 1780's. First, he sanctified his laws by contending, as we have already seen, that they were natural. If someone argued that this was not so, Restif simply shrugged his shoulders and complained that the disbeliever could not read nature properly. Second, he sanctified his laws with an absolute quality by appealing to the model of the hero Lycurgus. The Spartan legislator had enacted laws for his people which endured for centuries. Restif mistakenly asserted. He, Restif, had duplicated the simplicity, the grandeur, and elevated morality of Lycurgus and his laws should therefore be respected as were the ancient Greek's. But by the end of the eighteenth century, invoking the witness of nature and the model of the ancients was not convincing. New justifications for utopian theorizing were being formulated. Condorcet's ideal society was predicated upon the necessity of historical development; the nineteenth century would add the act of violent revolution to the list of justifications. The new legitimations of utopia—historical necessity and revolution—might not appeal to the Catholic traditionalist De Maistre, for whom only God could confer authority on human laws and social change, but they certainly had more popular force than Restif's arguments.

B. Static and Dynamic Ideals

Sir Thomas More imprinted a form upon the French conception of the ideal society that did not fade until the nineteenth century. More introduced his ideal world without locating it precisely; the island of Utopia lay somewhere in the New World, but the narrator had forgotten exactly where it was.[1] From the physical descriptions, the reader is led to think that utopia was really England. But More's vagueness in locating the island also implied that it could exist anywhere. Besides being geographically universal, Utopia was contemporary and it had a past. It was

---

[1] More, *Utopia*, ed. by Surtz (New Haven: Yale University Press, 1964), p. 6.

not a future expectation, envisioned as emerging in the course of historical development. In other words, More's ideal society was not limited to a particular people or place.

Thus More's conception of the institutions of Utopia bespoke a static, eternal society. Social change was insignificant, if not nonexistent. The utopians "have adopted such institutions of life as have laid the foundations of the commonwealth not only most happily, but also to last forever, as far as human prescience can forecast." [2] Utopia was a traditional, unchanging society in which laws and customs were passed down from generation to generation without the intrusion of any novelty. The simple, half-medieval, half-modern pattern of Utopian life maintained its even tenor of quiet serenity. As far as possible, even the population remained fixed, surplus Utopians being sent to colonize nearby lands.[3]

Restif also prescribed a static atmosphere for his ideal communities. Like More, his intention was to establish institutions that would be unchanging through time. In the play, L'An deux mille, a title Restif took from Mercier's L'An 2440, the life of utopians had not changed since the ideal laws were promulgated over two hundred years earlier.[4] Part of the conflict in the play results from Hardion's attempt to alter the fixed customs, an action that utopians considered a heinous crime. Expansion and growh were absolutely forbidden as well. The Statuts du Bourg d'Oudun limited the population to one hundred families. From More's Renaissance ideal to Restif's utopia formulated during the last years of the Old Regime, one trend of utopian thought envisioned the same static conditions as the perfect environment for man. The life of each utopian would embody a serene happiness—Restif termed it tranquility—that was secure against the uncertainties of the ravaging wheel of time.

By the end of the eighteenth century the static ideal was about to be displaced. As far back as Bacon's New Atlantis an alternative tradition of utopian thought had begun to emphasize inventions and novelty. The organization of inventions into a systematic endeavor constituted "science" and science was to be the vital principle of progress. A dynamic, ever-changing and ever-expanding utopia based on science needed a new theory of history. The dynamic utopias of the nineteenth century were to couple a view of science as a principle of expanding well-being with a progressist philosophy of history in which time moved in a straight line toward the perfection of humanity. In the eighteenth century, the

[2] Ibid., p. 151.
[3] Ibid., p. 76.
[4] Le Thesmographe, p. 519.

dream of a dynamic utopia was put forth by Turgot and received its clearest expression from his friend Condorcet.

Condorcet injected tension, movement, expansion, and growth into the utopian fantasy. What his editor called *Fragment sur l'Atlantide* (a commentary on Bacon's *New Atlantis*) together with his well-known *Esquisse d'un tableau historique des progrès de l'esprit humain* transformed the wish for tranquility into a vision of infinite movement. History was conceived as an almost unbending line of progress divided into ten epochs, the last of which defined the future. The *Esquisse* was composed during the turbulence of the revolution in 1793, while Condorcet hid from the Tribunal and the guillotine. The tone of his utopia captured the tensions of those emotionally charged days. Man's knowledge of nature, in the form of facts, constantly increased.[5] New combinations of sensations, churned through the mind of the genius-scientist, brought the facts to ever greater complexity and gave man ever more insight into nature's secrets. Fascination with inventions, so evident in the *Encyclopédie*, came to fruition with Condorcet who realized their significance for the progress of human society. Precursors like Mercier, who forecast the invention of malleable glass, transparent stone, inextinguishable lamps, and other gadgets [6] that we live with today did not, however, capture the new faith in science with Condorcet's clarity and grandeur. The advances of science in the Tenth Epoch could not even be forecast since the "infinite" accumulation of knowledge would increase "indefinitely." [7] In Condorcet's view, society was following the rocketing trajectory of history, which science had hammered into a straight, upward path. Hence he saw utopia as underpinned by a dynamic force which introduced change so rapidly that its consequences were unforseeable.

No trace of Condorcet's views of science and history can be found in Restif's utopian thought. Still, there was a dynamic principle in his utopia. Where Condorcet saw the expansion of knowledge leading to advances in technology that made movement the essence of society, Restif thought of man as an unstable, dynamic creature. Society, to Restif, was as rigid and unalterable as it was in More's ideal community. Its structure had to be immobile precisely because man's passions were volatile. The mechanical model of man as a sensory apparatus as in Condillac, La Mettrie, and Helvétius was continued in Condorcet's genius-scientist. This

---

[5] Condorcet, *Sketch for a Historical Picture of the Progress of the Human Mind*, trans. by J. Barraclough (London: Widenfeld and Nicolson, 1955), p. 185.

[6] Mercier, *op. cit.*, II, 61–87.

[7] Condorcet, *op. cit.*, p. 200.

man was a machine capable of calculating such values as an ethic of pleasure and pain and an epistemology of science. Restif's man was not so predictable, being at the mercy of passions that were in constant movement marked by violent eruptions. His utopian received sense impressions just as did Condorcet's utopian, but he reacted to them sensuously while Condorcet's recorded them in the scientist's laboratory. Restif, therefore, erected a perfect society which was so severely static that it could coerce the passions into tranquility, and make their expression tender instead of violent.

In terms of the static-dynamic dichotomy, Restif's utopia was transitional. It aimed at the older, Morean, static society but its inhabitants were dynamic, unstable people. More could picture utopian harmony and calm as attainable through a handful of simple laws, but Restif had to impose this harmony through hundreds of complex and rigidly repressive enactments. The Morean ideal of calm felicity was no longer seen as readily achievable by man if he could only rid himself of pride. Rather tranquility was produced by a frantic policeman who had to conjure up every conceivable means of coercion to maintain it.

The difference in tone between the static utopia of More and that of Restif is also evident in their writing. More was jesting, ironic, only half-serious about each of his proposals.[8] Book One of *Utopia* reflects his ambivalence by use of the dialogue form in which the author's view never emerges with clarity. There were always "ifs" and "buts," arguments both for and against. The *Idées singulières*, on the contrary, was written without any humor. The conglomeration of laws was inscribed on the utopian portals with absolute finality. Presumably all arguments that could ever be raised were refuted once and for all. After listing the regulations, Restif actually devoted a section in *Les Gynographes*, *L'Andrographe*, and *Le Thesmographe* to this purpose, calling it *Réponse aux Objections, sur chacun des Article du Projet de Règlement*.[9]

C. A Precursor of Fourier?

1. The Debate

Restif diverged furthest from the Morean tradition in his view of the place of love and the passions in the morality of utopia. The ideal for More was a balance of mental and physical activities.[10] But joys of the

---

[8] More, *op. cit.*, p. 36.
[9] *Le Thesmographe*, p. 5.
[10] More, *op. cit.*, p. 100.

flesh were quite subordinate to the pleasures of the spirit, specifically to humanist studies. Indeed, the Christian humanist saw health as the greatest bodily pleasure. His grudging acceptance of sensate pleasure condoned only "clearly perceptible sweetness." The range of bodily pleasures was decidedly narrow. "This agreeable sensation occurs when we discharge feces from our bowels or perform the activity generative of children or relieve the itching of some part by rubbing or scratching." [11] Nothing could be farther from Restif's affirmation of love and its intimate connection with the vital forces of life than More's notion of the equal value of excretion, scratching and copulation. There is an unbridgeable gap between the predominantly contemplative ideal of More's perfect society and Restif's rehabilitation of the flesh.

For his revaluation of the passions, Restif has been regarded in the history of utopian thought as a precursor of Fourier. In the early nineteenth century, during the savage struggle between the great systems of Fourier and Saint-Simon, later joined by Comte, Proudhon, and Marx, Pierre Leroux, a Saint-Simonian, attempted to undercut the Fourierists in his journal *Revue Sociale*. His *"Lettres sur le Fouriérisme,"* which continued through most of the short life of the journal from 1846 to 1850, pointed a Saint-Simonian blade at the heart of the opponent's system. With articles on Rabelais, Fénelon, Diderot, Restif, and anyone who could be marshaled to the fray, Leroux thrust upon Fourier the charge of plagiarism. The giants of utopian socialism, the prophets who contested for the support of the alienated, watched Leroux blast his enemy point for point and vision for vision by draging out Restif's dusty books. "You have read in my preceding letters on Fourier that I accused him quite pointedly of having taken, without acknowledging it, his *physique* and his cosmogony from Rétif, his ethics from the same Rétif and from Diderot . . ." [12] Leroux's suit amounted to this: without once mentioning Restif's name, Fourier had adopted and elaborated the essence of his utopian thought, the cosmogony and the religoin of sensual pleasures. Restif was thus the seminal genius and Fourier the second-rate hack. The Saint-Simonian's argument is important and it has been reiterated by most scholars who have written on Restif. [13]

[11] *Ibid.*, p. 99.

[12] Pierre Leroux, "Lettres sur le Fouriérisme," *Revue Sociale* (March, 1950), p. 103.

[13] I. Bloch, *Rétif de la Bretonne: der Mensch, der Schriftsteller, der Reformator* (Berlin: Harrwitz, 1906), p. 497; H. Girsberger, *Der utopische Sozialismus des 18. Jahrhunderts in Frankreich und seine philosophischen und materiellen Grundlagen* (Zurich: Rascher, 1924), pp. 187–188; H. Tuzet, "Deux types de cosmogonies vitalis-

The charge against Fourier of intellectual plagiarism has been expanded through the years to include Restif's ideas on association, the phalanstery, and even women. Since Fourier's utopia is among the handful of truly novel visions and has had great influence on many thinkers, Restif's reputation would be considerably enhanced if the charge could be sustained. It is a likely that Fourier did read Restif since the bookshops were full of his unsold volumes during Fourier's youth at the end of the eighteenth century. But as Fourier never mentioned Restif, their ideas must be compared individually in order to test Leroux's charge. It should be noted that Bourgin, in his classic study of Fourier, has denied outright Restif's paternity of the utopia of passionate attraction.[14] Opinions are sharply divided and any conclusion must answer the objections of both sides of the debate.

2. The Cosmogonies

Both geniuses made part of their utopian projects a study of "the mysterious harmony of the celestial spheres." The most extraordinary pages of their extraordinary writings concern their cosmogonies. It is not surprising that in this extreme manifestation of their thought they would be most similar.[15] Fourier, like Restif, unveiled nature's secrets in terms of the sexual passions. "Female planets, being androgynous like male planets, copulate with themselves and with other female planets. Thus, the Earth, by copulating with itself, by the fusion of its two typical aromas [fluids], the masculine toward the north pole and the feminine toward the south pole, engenders the *Cerisier*, a subpivotal fruit of the red fruits. . . ."[16] Let us not try to explain Fourier's eccentric terminology. Both he and Restif imagined the whole universe alive and with parts interrelated. While Restif pictured the cosmos as an animal, Fourier favored the vegetable kingdom: "our universe is like a

tes," *Revue des sciences humaines*, 1961, N.S.F. 101, p. 40; A. Lichtenberger, *Le Socialisme au XVIIIe siècle* (Paris: Alcan, 1895), p. 219; B. Malon, "Rétif de la Bretonne," *Revue socialiste*, IX, No 54 (June, 1889), p. 661; A. Viatte, *Les Sources occultes du romantisme* (Paris: Champion, 1928), p. 265. Only the most important commentators are listed.

[14] Hubert Bourgin, *Fourier: contribution à l'étude du socialisme française* (Paris: Société nouvelle de librairie et d'édition, 1905), pp. 77, 81, 134.

[15] See the two articles by H. Tuzet: on Restif, *op. cit.*; on Fourier, "Deux types de cosmogonies vitalistes: 2. Charles Fourier, hygieniste du cosmos," *Revue des sciences humaines*, N. Sér. F. 101 (1961), pp. 37–47.

[16] Charles Fourier, *Oeuvres complètes, Théorie de l'unité universelle* (Paris: Bureaux de la Phalange, 1841), III, 244.

sidereal apple." [17] Restif's universe of bears, apes, and goats was transformed into one of melons, carrots, and peaches.[18]

The parallels between their amusing aberrations go much further. For both utopians there was a fundamental principle which was the essence of the cosmos: the passions. Newton's law of gravitation became, in their hands, a kind of libido which was the motive force of all actions (physical, social, and moral) and which in its variations gave different colorations to all beings.[19] Their special intention was to show the interrelatedness of all spheres of life through the passions, a project which Fourier carried out with "scientific" precision through his endless categories. Like Restif, Fourier perceived that there was an economy of the passions,[20] so that the vitality of a given people was finite and dependent upon both the climate of their specific location and the copulation of the earth with the sun and, for Fourier, the surrounding planets. Incidentally, each invented extra planets to fit the specifications of his system,[21] hardly in the best scientific tradition. More prominently in Fourier's cosmogony than in Restif's, God conducted the vast sexual interplay of the heavenly globes by controlling the distribution of the passions.

Furthermore, neither of them could settle for a materialistic metaphysic. Fourier actually spoke of a soul; Restif so fused the soul with matter that they were indistinguishable; both thought the soul was immortal.[22] Also, a strange doctrine of evolution was part of their cosmogonies. After creation, Fourier agreed with Restif, there were many species of men, among which were the "Patagons," Australian giants, superior to all others.[23] Placing a superior being among the first men and implying that the history of man was a steady degeneration from the early high point was an old habit of thought that the utopians could not escape but to which they contributed a novel flavor. Finally, the affinities of these doctrines to ancient mythologies was recognized by both utopians. Fourier praised "the barbarians and the savages," who "in their crude fables" far surpassed the most rational modern systems.[24] A habit of attacking the dominant scientific thought of the eighteenth

[17] Ibid., p. 262.
[18] See F. E. Manuel, Prophets of Paris (New York: Harper Torchbook, 1965), pp. 243–248, for a discussion of Fourier's ambivalent feelings about his cosmos.
[19] Fourier, op. cit., III, 256.
[20] Ibid., III, 311.
[21] Tuzet, op. cit., 1961, p. 37.
[22] La Découverte australe, III, 510; Tuzet, op. cit., 1961, p. 40.
[23] Fourier, op. cit., I, 76.
[24] Ibid., III, 305.

century was prevalent in both thinkers. Their ideal societies were thus grounded upon imaginative, vitalist cosmogonies.

The cosmic notions of both Restif and Fourier were obvious projections and their personalities can be found displayed in their maps of the stars. The visions of the lonely salesman depict an ebulliently sensate cosmos, complementing his frustrated emotional warmth. Restif's images were darker and became less optimistic as the years passed. But with him too the universe turned on the excited sensuality that remained thwarted during his walks through the streets of Paris. Fourier's cosmogony was neater, more precise, more systematic and more comprehensively worked out; Restif's was disorganized, menacing and unlawful, like a monster. By their strongly sensual qualities, in which everything pulls toward everything else, both cosmogonies reflect men with divided hearts, at war with themselves. If Fourier's cosmos was an act of aggression toward the philosophical authorities,[25] Restif's was a validation of the morality of his sensual nature. Whatever interpretation is given to their theories of the universe, the similarities between them are too prominent to be overlooked. It is impossible to prove that Fourier was directly influenced by Restif, but their cosmogonies demonstrate at least that they spoke from remarkably proximate intellectual climates.

3. The Passions

The passions were the life blood of Restif's and Fourier's ideal societies. They were, for both, cosmic energies whose universal conditions were related to the movement of society. Life and history were equally shaped by a grand arc of change in the distribution of energy in the universe. In Restif's system, planets, being alive, went through a life cycle; the death of the earth would terminate the evolution of all civilizations. Man was a product of this evolutionary wheel and his nature was shaped by climate, a given intensity of solar energy. In Fourier's system, the universal movement and the social system of passionate attraction evolved and would terminate together. For the earth, the end would come after 80,000 years; within that span a mere 5,000 years encompassed a seven-period cycle of which our civilization was only the fifth stage!

Restif emphasized the biological nature of the passions, whereas Fourier stressed their psychological nature. With the Romantic's fascination for variety and diversity, Fourier organized phalansteries for 810 human types based on different combinations of twelve "pure" passions. Social functions of work and administration would be voluntarily discharged by

[25] Manuel, op. cit., p. 244.

appropriate passionate types as an expression of those types. Moralists, Fourier asserted, condemned the vast majority of people because civilization did not make good use of their passionate natures. The *Papillon* (butterfly) [26] who could not maintain enduring relationships, the *Cabaliste*, who sought intrigues and fashioned plots, would have functions in utopia. To denigrate these types as morally inferior, to deny the validity of the desires of the *Papillon* and *Cabaliste* was to Fourier an arbitrary restriction of human variety. Where Restif called for the repression of one half of the passions, the destructive ones, Fourier demanded the fulfillment of each and every passion of which humanity was capable. In fact, Fourier denied that the destructive passions were real; he contended that they were products of a misguided civilization, not essential to human nature.

Both blamed civilization for corrupting man's passionate nature. In Fourier's view, if there were passions for poverty and persecution civilization could be accepted and justified.[27] But these indignities were artificial products of an imperfect stage of social development. Boredom was the characteristic mood of man in civilization, and it punctuated the failure of civilization to account for man's needs since it denoted a low intensity of the passions.[28] Restif's notion of satiation was similar to Fourier's idea of boredom except satiation was the vice of too much freedom while boredom emanated from the narrowness of civilized pleasures. The phalanstery would assure that the perfect combination of passionate types were grouped together. Complementary needs would cancel each other out and there would be a few frustrated passions when one representative of each human type inhabited the phalanstery. Organization replaced Restif's repression as the means to attain harmonious passionate attraction. Fourier tore down the barriers of human experience that Restif had endeavored to fortify with greater strength. Happiness in the phalanstery was immediate sensate gratification, a form of happiness Restif deemed impossible when he encountered it in Sade's cruel orgies. For Fourier was more like Rousseau in the early *Discours*, finding the principle of evil in society, while Restif resembled Rousseau in

[26] Gérard de Nerval found in *Le Pornographe*, *le papillon* as a human type. He claimed that Restif saw *la papillone* as the law of organization of many institutions, *Les Illuminés* (Paris: Champion, 1929), p. 204. Gérard further argued that Fourier took the idea from Restif. I found no mention of *le papillon* in *Le Pornographe* and if it was mentioned it did not play a significant role in Restif's utopia.

[27] Fourier, *The Passions of the Human Soul*, trans. by J. Morell (London: Bailliere, 1851), p. 11.

[28] *Ibid.*, p. 8.

the *Contrat social* in which human nature was imperfect and required social restraints.

Restif's idea of association was therefore only superficially like Fourier's. In his brief utopian codes Restif never considered personality types as a principle of social organization. Although he described the passions with richness and variety in his novels, especially in the hundreds of short stories or episodes in *Les Contemporaines,* he was too deeply embedded in the eighteenth century to define the essence of man as variety. Restif's emphasis, compared to Fourier's, remained on the underlying unity and similarity of members of the human race. Where Restif did draw the line, at the biological determinants of age and sex, Fourier erased the markings. Feminine equality was basic to the phalanstery since, psychologically, a given woman might be identical to a man.

In this comparison of the utopian thought of Restif and Fourier it was necessary to emphasizee the differences between them. Generally speaking, the similarities in interest and the parallels in conception are astonishing. It would be difficult to deny a direct line of intellectual transmission from Restif to Fourier. The cosmogonies, the rehabilitation of the passions, the elements of socialism, all evoke the same conclusion. What Restif envisioned in rough outline, Fourier developed in great detail and rigorous, if often absurd, logic. The libertine-moralist who invented utopias as a supplement to his novels in the eighteenth century became, in the nineteenth century, the professional prophet, with a doctrine and a following, devoting his energies exclusively to his vision while waiting for a converted world to knock at his door. The precise determinants of the transmission are not clear: did Fourier read Restif or was the similarity an effect of the intellectual climate or *zeitgeist?* Oral transmission was unlikely because the *Idées singulières* were not widely read. (Benjamin Franklin was the only person of note who is known to have read *L'Andrographe.*) In fact, with the possible exception of Fourier, no significant influence can be claimed for Restif's utopias. In the utopian tradition, his interest consists in the original and often paradoxical character of the detailed formulation of his ideas, not in their impact on others. Fourier's utopia, on the other hand, was the comprehensive formulation of a novel vision that, after the fact, we can see gestating in Restif's thought.

D. THE TRANSITIONAL VISION

The utopia of a moralist, Restif's ideal society was thoroughly of his century. His specific utopian values tended to reflect his reaction against the Enlightenment and to anticipate Romantic strains of thought. Their theoretical framework—utilitarianism, nature as the matrix of social law, happiness as virtue—derived from the moral thought of the eighteenth century. In tone, Restif's utopia was Morean and could be described as the last utopia of the Morean tradition, although, as we have seen, it also foreshadowed Fourier. Hence Restif's utopia was transitional, half old, half new, as much an end as a beginning, equally old-fashioned and avant-garde.

The Romantic tones of Restif's thought suggest his debt to Rousseau. The great impact of Rousseau's writing on Restif has been pointed out in several places in this study. It might be said that Rousseau formulated a new intellectual outlook, an emotional naturalism [29] that drove the Enlightenment in a new direction—questioning civilization but not dismissing it, calling for a revaluation of the emotions without giving up reason completely—and that Restif found this new outlook compelling and wrote his utopias within it. If Rousseau found his warmest welcome in Germany in the eighteenth century, Restif was his rare French advocate. In a general sense, Restif wrote the utopias that Rousseau never penned; he gave Rousseau's world view its concrete utopian expression.

Yet the polar nature of Restif's utopian thought, which has been emphasized throughout this study, signaled a new direction in the history of ideal societies. Whereas the utopias of French thinkers of the Old Regime projected a deep-rooted emotional balance in the author's attitude toward utopia as well as in the ideal values themselves, the tone began with Restif to become more urgent, the values less harmonious, and the atmosphere of utopia more tense. Restif's vision of utopia ushered in a new uneasiness for although his ideas operated within familiar eigtheenth-century modes, his polar sensibility gave them a new emotional dimension. If Morelly devised one repressive and one permissive utopia, Restif, in the *Idées singulières* and *La Découverte australe par un homme volant*, heightened the tension to the furthest possible limit to all or nothing.

The utopia of the corrupted peasant anticipated the nineteenth century in another important way. As we have noted, Restif's eye, as he wrote regulation after regulation, was focused on *le peuple;* the peasants, the journeymen, and the transient workers of the towns. The stage of history was extended to include the dark beasts from the lower orders. Restif did not celebrate the suffering of the exploited classes, but he knew *le peuple* and he fashioned his utopian laws according to its needs. In this

[29] See Irving Babbitt, *Rousseau and Romanticism* (Cleveland: Meridian, 1966).

respect he was a true socialist. Although his image of the people was not clouded by the Romantic nostalgia of Michelet, neither was it dimmed by the distant focus of La Bruyère. The lower orders entered utopia through Restif's pen neither by reason of an ideological expression of the dominant social class nor as the reaction to that expression by the "true consciousness" of the revolutionary. Restif's utopia for the people was not a compliment to their humanity and not a glorification of their suffering, but the realistic appraisal of a man who prided himself on an indelicate intimacy with the man of the street.

Bibliography

Restif's fate in the European intellectual and literary tradition has been uneven. Except for a minor flurry of interest in the mid-1780's, following the publication of *Le Paysan perverti*, contemporary Frenchmen either scorned or ignored Restif. It was rather the eighteenth-century Germans—Goethe, Schiller, W. von Humboldt—who looked seriously at his major works, notably *Monsieur Nicolas*. To them, Restif had broken the rules of the century and therefore he was found interesting. His friend, the poet Cubières-Palmézeaux, in *Notice historique et critique sur la vie et les ouvrages de N.-E. Restif de la Bretonne* (1811), was the only contemporary to record his impressions at any length. This neglect doubtless explains the loss of almost all Restif's manuscripts.

During the nineteenth century, his obscurity deepened. Only chance encounters by a handful of Frenchmen disturbed what appeared to be his permanent burial in intellectual oblivion. Then, at midcentury, Leroux resurrected Restif in his "Lettres sur le Fouriérisme," *Revue Sociale*, March 1850, pp. 103–107, positing his influence on Fourier. Shortly later, a pioneer study was made by Charles Monselet, *Restif de la Bretonne: Sa vie et ses amours* (Paris: Aubry, 1854). Paul Lacroix's unreliable *Bibliographie et iconographie de tous les ouvrages de Restif de la Bretonne* (Paris: Fontaine, 1875) was the last important work of the century.

It would not be an overstatement to say that the twentieth century has resurrected Restif. Perhaps more than anything else, the shift in the climate of opinion away from formal literary language and toward descriptions of sexual relations has made Restif's belated arrival possible. The prejudices of an aristocratic culture that dominated French scholarship until recent times were sufficient to preclude a fair assessment of his worth. French critics and moralists have now taken a closer look at the peasant who was able to express the passions so directly. Restif is being read not only as an acute psychologist of the passions, but also as a stylist who broadened the French language with concrete and popular expressions. An important and still serviceable study by Iwan Bloch, *Rétif de la Bretonne: der Mensch, der Schriftsteller, der Reformator* (Berlin: Harrwitz, 1906), was symptomatic of the new mood. Other studies are those of Frantz Funck-Brentano, *Rétif de la Bretonne inconnu* (Paris: Margraff, 1927); Adolphe Tabarant, *Le Vrai visage de Rétif de la Bretonne* (Paris: Editions Montaigne, 1936); and the first work in English, C. R. Dawes, *Restif de la Bretonne* (London: Whitefriars, 1946). Two studies followed which attempted to clarify the existing state of scholarship: Armand Bégué, *Etat présent des études sur Rétif de la Bretonne* (Paris: Belles Lettres, 1948), and the excellent bibliography by J. Rives Childs, *Restif de la Bretonne* (Paris: Briffaut, 1949). Marc Chadourne's fine study, *Restif de la Bretonne, ou le Siècle prophétique* (Paris: Hachette, 1958), places Restif in the romantic tradition. Most recently Charles Porter, *Restif's Novels* (New Haven: Yale University Press, 1967), sets out for the first time a systematic study of all Restif's novels and includes a good bibliography, taking up where Childs left off.

With all this interest in Restif's life and novels, there has not been a comprehensive treatment of his utopias. The reasons for the neglect are plain. The *Idées singulières* is difficult to obtain and tedious to read. Most scholars have preferred to look at the philosophical sections of *Monsieur Nicolas* and the occasional presentation of ideas in *Les Nuits de Paris*. The few studies that have been made on Restif's utopias have all followed the misleading precedent set by Leroux of approaching the task from the perspective of nineteenth-century socialism. André Lichtenberger, *Le Socialisme au XVIIIe siècle* (Paris: Alcan, 1895), Hans Girsberger, *Der utopische Sozialismus des 18. Jahrhunderts in Frankreich und seine philosophischen und materiellen Grundlagen* (Zurich: Rascher, 1924), and A. R. Ioannisiani, "Restif de la Bretonne et le Communisme utopique," *La Pensée*, March–April 1958, pp. 91–103, have failed to disclose a complete picture of Restif's thought for this reason. My study has attempted to take a fresh look at Restif's utopian thought within the context of the utopian tradition and within the framework of the ethical thought of the eighteenth century.

Several recent articles on special aspects of Restif's thought are worthy of mention. Jacques Pinset, "Les Origines instinctives de la révolution française," *Revue d'histoire économique et sociale*, XXXIX (1961), pp. 198–228, is helpful in establishing Restif's peculiar perspective on the events of the revolution. C. A. Porter, "Restif, Rousseau and *Monsieur Nicolas*," *Romantic Review*, LIV (Dec. 1963), pp. 262–273, recognizes the influence of Rousseau in the *Idées singulières*. Finally, Hélène Tuzet, "Deux types de cosmogonies vitalistes: Restif de la Bretonne ou le coeur humain dévoilé," *Revue des sciences humaines*, N. Sér. Fasc. 100 (1960), pp. 495–506, is an incisive analysis of Restif's cosmogony.

WORKS BY RESTIF DE LA BRETONNE

Collected Editions

L'Oeuvre de Restif de la Bretonne, ed. by B. de Villeneuve (Paris: Biblio. des curieux, 1911).

Collection des plus belles pages de Restif de la Bretonne (Paris: Société du Mercure de France, 1925).

L'Oeuvre de Restif de la Bretonne, ed. by Henry Bachlin (Paris: Editions du Trianon, 1930–1932), 9 vols. The value of this collection is greatly reduced as it does not include a complete reprint of any of Restif's works.

Restif de la Bretonne, preface by F. Marceau (Paris: Mercure de France, 1964).

Individual Works, with Selected Reprints and Translations

La Famille vertueuse, Lettres traduites de l'anglais (Paris: Duchesne, 1767), 4 vols.

Lucile, ou Les Progrès de la vertue (Paris: Delalain, 1768).

Le Pied de Fanchette, ou L'Orphéline française (Paris: Humblot, 1769), 3 vols.

La Confidence nécessaire, Lettres de Lord Austin de N . . . , à Lord Humfrey de Dorset, son ami (London: Nourse and Snelling, 1769), 2 vols.

La Fille naturelle (Paris: Humblot, 1769), 2 vols.

Le Pornographe, ou Idées d'un honnête-homme sur un projet de règlement pour les prostituées (The Hague: Gosse and Pinet, 1770).

La Mimographe, ou Idées d'un honnête-femme pour la réformation du théâtre national (Amsterdam, 1770).

Le Marquis de T . . . (Tavan), ou L'Ecole de la jeunesse (Paris: Le Jay, 1771).

Adèle de Com . . . (Comminge), ou Lettres d'une fille à son père (Paris: Edme, 1772), 5 vols.

La Femme dans les trois états de fille, d'épouse et de mère, Histoire morale, comique et véritable (Paris: De-Hansy, 1773), 3 vols.

Le Ménage parisien, ou Déliée et Sotentout (The Hague, 1773), 2 vols.

Les Nouveaux mémoires d'un homme-de-qualité (Paris: Duchesne, 1774).

Le Paysan perverti, ou Les Dangers de la ville (1775), 4 vols.

Le Fin-Matois, ou Histoire du Grand-Taquin (The Hague, 1776), 3 vols.

Le Nouvel Emile, ou l'Education pratique (Paris: Costard, 1770–1776), 4 vols. Also published under the title *L'Ecole des pères.*

Les Gynographes, ou Idées de deux honnêtes-femmes sur un project de règlement, proposé à toute l'Europe, pour mettre les femmes à leur place, et opérer le bonheur des deux sexes (Paris: Humblot, 1777).

Le Quadragénaire, ou L'Age de renoncer aux passions (Paris: Duchesne, 1777), 2 vols.

Le Nouvel Abeilard, ou Lettres de deux amans qui ne se sont jamais vus (Paris: Duchesne, 1778).

La Vie de mon père (Paris: Duchesne, 1779), 2 vols.

Les Faiblesses d'une jolie femme (1780).

La Malédiction paternelle (Paris: Duchesne, 1780), 3 vols.

Les Contemporaines, 42 vols., published in 3 series. Reprinted Selections (Paris: Marpon and Flammarion, 1875), 3 vols.

  1. *Les Contemporaines, ou Avantures des plus jolies femmes de l'âge présent* (Paris: Belin, 1780–1782), 17 vols. Reprint by Paris: A. Michel, 1910, 1 vol.

  2. *Les Contemporaines-du-Commun, ou Avantures des belles marchandes* (Leipzig: Büschel, 1782–1783), 13 vols. Reprint by Paris: M. Glomeau, 1927, 1 vol.

  3. *Les Contemporaines-par-Gradation, ou Avantures des jolies-femmes de l'âge actuel suivant la gradation des principaux états de la société* (Paris: Duchesne, 1783), 12 vols.

La Découverte australe par un homme-volant, ou Le Dédale français (Paris: 1781), 4 vols.

L'Andrographe, ou Idées d'un honnête-homme, sur un projet de règlement, proposé à toutes les nations de l'Europe, pour opérer une réforme générale des moeurs, et par elle, le bonheur du genre humain (Paris: Duchesne, 1782).

La Dernière avanture d'un homme de quarante-cinq ans (Paris: Regnault, 1783).

La Prévention nationale (Paris: Regnault, 1784).

La Paysanne pervertie, ou Les Dangers de la ville (Paris: Duchesne, 1784), 4 vols.

Le Paysan et la paysane pervertis (The Hague, 1784), 4 vols.

Les Veillées du Marais, ou Histoire du Grand Prince Oribeau (1785), 2 vols.

Les Françaises (Paris: Guillot, 1786), 4 vols.

Les Parisiennes (Paris: Guillot, 1787), 4 vols.

Tableaux de la vie (Strasbourg: Trenttel, 1787), 2 vols.

Les Nuits de Paris, ou Le Spectateur nocturne (Paris: 1788–1794), 8 vols.

La Femme infidelle (Paris: Maradan, 1788), 4 vols.

Ingénue saxancour, ou La Femme séparée (Paris: Maradan, 1789), 3 vols.

Le Thesmographe, ou Idées d'un honnêe-homme, sur un projet de règlement, proposé à toutes les nations de l'Europe, pour opérer une réforme générale des loix (Paris: Maradan, 1789).

Monument du costume physique et moral de la fin du dix-huitième siècle (Neuwied sur le Rhin: Société typographique, 1789).

Le Palais Royal (Paris: Guillot, 1790), 3 vols.

L'Année des dames nationales (Paris, 1791–1794), 12 vols. Also published as *Les Provinciales*.

Le Drame de la vie (Paris: Duchesne, 1793), 5 vols.

Théâtre de Restif de la Bretonne (Paris: Duchesne and Merigot, 1793), 5 vols.

Monsieur Nicolas, ou Le Coeur-humain dévoilé (Paris: by himself, 1794–1797), 16 vols. The standard edition is by Pauvert (Paris: Tuileries, 1959), 6 vols.

Philosophie de Monsieur Nicolas (Paris: Cercle-sociale, 1796), 3 vols.

L'Anti-Justine, ou Les Délices de l'amour (Paris: Girouard, 1798).

Les Posthumes, Lettres reçues après la mort du Mari, par sa femme, qui le croit à Florence (Paris: Duchesne, 1802), 4 vols.

Les Nouvelles contemporaines, ou Histoires de quelques femmes du jour (Paris: Société typographique, 1802), 2 vols.

Published Posthumously

Histoire des compagnes de Maria (Paris: Guillaume, 1811), 3 vols. The first volume is a biography by Cubières-Palmézeaux, a friend of Restif.

Lettres inédites de Restif de la Bretonne (Nantes: Forest and Grimaud, 1883).

Mes inscriptions, ed. by Paul Cottin (Paris: Bibliothèque Elzevirienne, 1889).

WORKS ABOUT RESTIF DE LA BRETONNE

Bibliographies

Bégué, Armand, *Etat présent des études sur Rétif de la Bretonne* (Paris: Belles Lettres, 1948).

Bloch, Iwan, *Rétif-Bibliothek* (Berlin, 1906).

Bordes de Fortage, *Notice sur la vie et les ouvrages de Rétif de la Bretonne* (Bordeaux, 1927).

Childs, James Rives, *Restif de la Bretonne* (Paris: Briffaut, 1949). This is a fine work of scholarship and it should be consulted for all questions concerning reprints and translations.

Courbin, Jean Claude, *Restif et son oeuvre* (Paris: Rousseau-Girard, 1959).
L'Enfer de la Bibliothèque Nationale by G. Apollinaire, F. Fleuret and L. Perceau, 1913. Good for *L'Anti-Justine*.
Lacroix, Paul, *Bibliographie et iconographie de tous les ouvrages de Restif de la Bretonne* (Paris: A. Fontaine, 1875). A standard.
Schurig, Arthur, *Rétif de la Bretonne, Katalog einer Sammlung seiner Werke* (Berlin: Antiquariat am Lützowplatz, 1922).

Full Studies of Restif de la Bretonne

Barras, Louis, *Le Fétichisme: Restif de la Bretonne fut-il fétichiste?* (Thèse soutenue devant la Faculté de Médicine de Montpellier, 1913).
Bégué, Armand, *Etat présent des études sur Rétif de la Bretonne* (Paris: Belles Lettres, 1948). A summary of existing scholarship, with a good chapter on historiography.
Bloch, Iwan, *Rétif de la Bretonne: der Mensch, der Schriftsteller, der Reformator* (Berlin: Harrwitz, 1906). There is a short final chapter on Restif's utopia which is suggestive.
Boissin, Firmin, *Restif de La Bretonne* (Paris: Daffis, 1875).
Chadourne, Marc, *Restif de La Bretonne, ou Le Siécle prophétique* (Paris: Hachette, 1958). An excellent new biography by a novelist and scholar.
Charpentier, Dr. Louis, *Restif de la Bretonne, sa perversion fétichiste* (Bordeaux, 1912).
Courbin, J. Cl., *Le Monde de Rétif* (Paris: Rousseau-Girard, 1962), 44 pp.
Dawes, C. R., *Restif de La Bretonne, 1734–1806* (London: Whitefriars, 1946). Short and adequate biography, the first in English.
Funck-Brentano, Frantz, *Rétif de la Bretonne: Portraits et documents inédits* (Paris: A. Michel, 1928). An overly sympathetic biography.
Grasilier, Léonce, *Rétif de la Bretonne inconnu* (Paris: Margraff, 1927). A minor book about Restif's employment with the police. The authenticity of the documents he uses has been questioned.
Martin, Angus Andrews, *La Peinture de la réalité parisienne dans les romans de Restif de la Bretonne* (Thèse, Université de Paris, 1961).
Mireur, Dr. H., *Notes historiques et justificatives et étude critique pour une édition du Porno-graphe* (Bruxelles, 1899).
Monselet, Chas., *Rétif de la Bretonne: Sa vie et ses amours; documents inédits; ses malheurs, sa vieillesse et sa mort; ce qui a été écrit sur lui; ses descendants; catalogue complet et detaillé de ses ouvrages, suivi de quelques extraits* (Paris: Aubry, 1854). First authoritative study of Restif and a standard through the nineteenth century.
Naughton, Alexandre, *Le Tableau des moeurs dans les romans de Rétif de la Bretonne* (Paris: Les Presses modernes, 1929).
Porter, Charles, *Restif's Novels, or An Autobiography in Search of an Author* (New Haven: Yale Univ. Press, 1966).
Schurig, Arthur, *Restif de la Bretonne: Aus dem Leben und den Büchern eines Erotomanen* (Paris: Vincennes, 1906).
Tabarant, Adolphe, *Le Vrai visage de Rétif de la Bretonne* (Paris: Editions Montaigne, 1936). At the start of Tabarant this life-and-works study, was unsympathetic to Restif and unwilling to accept anything without rigorous proof. The book has been subject to controversy.

Vaudoyer, Jean Louis, *Paris au XVIIIe siècle, Restif de la Bretonne, Le Paris populaire* (Paris: Musée Carnavalet, 1934–1935). A catalogue of an exhibition on Restif's 200th birthday. Good for information about Binet's prints.

Selected Articles

Ambrières, Francis, "Tabarant, le vrai visage de Restif de la Bretonne," *Nouvelles littéraires artistiques et scientifiques*, 1936.

Anon., "Paris by Night," *Times Literary Supplement*, No. 60 (Oct. 27, 1961), pp. 761–763. An essay in response to a one-volume reprint of *Les Nuits de Paris*.

Anon., "The Salon and the Bawdy-house," *Times Literary Supplement*, No. 61 (July 6, 1962), p. 492. A review of the Pauvert edition of *Monsieur Nicolas*.

Assézat, J., "Rétif de la Bretonne," *Realisme*, Jan. 15, 1857. By one of the finest nineteenth-century scholars of Restif.

Auriant, "Monsieur Nicolas et la belle Guéant, ou Les mensonges de Restif dévoilés," *Aesculape*, année 35 (1954), pp. 89–104. Concerns a love affair of Restif with an actress, questioning his alleged successes.

Aury, Dominique, "On dévore du Restif," *La Nouvelle nouvelle revue française*, année 7 (1959), pp. 690–696. A short sketch of Restif.

Bachelin, Henri, "Restif de la Bretonne, écrivain et moraliste," *Hippocrate*, No. 7 (Sept., 1934), pp. 634–647. Heckles French literary critics for not recognizing Restif's merits.

Barjac, Claude, "Tabarant, le vrai visage de Restif de la Bretonne," *Le Larousse mensuel illustré*, tome X, No. 363 (May, 1937).

Bédé, J. A., "Restif de la Bretonne; ou, Le Siècle prophétique, by M. Chadourne," *Romantic Review*, No. 51 (Feb., 1960), pp. 53–59. A very complimentary verdict.

Bégué, Armand, "La critique des moeurs dans les oeuvres de Rétif de la Bretonne," *Romantic Review*, Vol. 29 (1938), pp. 243–252. Sees Retif's utopianism as basically communist.

———, "Tabarant, le vrai visage de Restif de la Bretonne," *Romantic Review*, Vol. 28 (Feb., 1937), pp. 79–82. Criticizes the organization of Tabarant's book.

Bellessort, A., "Rétif de la Bretonne, de F. Funck-Brentano," *Journal des Débats*, No. 35 (Sept. 14, 1928), pp. 438–443. A witness to the sudden increase in Restif's popularity in France.

Berthoud, Samuel-Henri, "Causeries sur la littérature et les arts: Restif de la Bretonne," *La Presse*, Sept. 4, 1836. By a grandchild of Restif.

Beuchot, A., "Notice nécrologique sur Restif de la Bretonne," *Le Décade, revue philosophique littéraire, politique*, Vol. II (April 11, 1806), pp. 120–126. Includes a list, with many errors, of Restif's works.

Bourget, P., "Une vie de paysan sous l'ancien régime," *Revue des Deux Mondes*, 7 pér. (Oct. 1, 1928), pp. 699–709. Uses Restif to counter arguments that the French Revolution was a response to economic misery.

Brunetière, Ferdinand, "Les Origines du roman naturaliste," *Revue des Deux Mondes*, année 51 (Sept., 1881), pp. 438–450. This eminent critic finds Restif's novels vulgar.

Chadourne, Marc, "Eros and Restif," *Yale French Studies*, No. 11 (1953), pp. 12–17. Sees Eros as partly sensual, partly dream-like.

——, "Restif de la Bretonne, prophet and precursor," *American Society Legion of Honor Magazine*, Vol. 27 (1957), pp. 345–359. Restif's concept of time is similar to Proust's.

——, "Restif de la Bretonne revisité," *Revue de Paris*, année 64 (July, 1957), pp. 20–31. Put together from bits of his book.

Charpentier, Dr. Louis, "Restif de la Bretonne, étude psychopathologique," *Hippocrate*, No. 7 (Sept., 1934), pp. 577–604. An outline of Restif's psychic ills.

Chinard, Gilbert, "An Eighteenth-Century Interpretation of the 'Struggle for Existence,' Restif de la Bretonne's Ecole des Pères," *Proceedings of the American Philosophical Society*, Vol. 102 (1958), pp. 547–554. Sees Restif's application of the idea of struggle to society as novel.

Cornevin, Maurice, "Un Curieux romancier du XVIIIe siècle, habitant de la Montagne Sainte Geneviève: Restif de la Bretonne," *La Montagne Sainte Geneviève et ses abords*, No. 25 (1957), 6 pp.

Courbin, J.-Cl., "Encore un mot sur Restif," *Bulletin du bibliophile et du bibliothécaire*, No. 2 (1962), pp. 96–106.

——, "Le Plus fort des pamphlets: ou ouvrage peu connu de Rétif," *Bulletin du bibliophile et du bibliothécaire*, No. 2 (1960), pp. 69–75. Argues convincingly against Tabarant that this is really a work of Restif.

——, "A propos d'un texte inconnu sur Restif de la Bretonne," *Bulletin du bibliophile et du bibliothécaire*, No. 3 (1959), pp. 93–101. Claims that "Les historiettes du jour, ou Paris tel qu' il est," by M. Nougaret (Paris: Duchesne, 1787) is really by Restif.

Dangon, Georges, "Sur un sujet inépuisé concernant un homme inépuisable, 'Monsieur Nicolas' Restif de la Bretonne," *Le Courrier graphique*, année 3, (1938), pp. 3–13. On Restif as printer.

Desfeuilles, André, "Le Griffon de l'île Saint-Louis," *Bulletin de la Société archéologique, historique et artistique*, Fasc. 208 (1964), pp. 56–57.

Fabureau, H., "Une émule de Rétif de la Bretonne: la comtesse de Choiseul," *Mercure de France*, No. 309 (May, 1950), pp. 188–191.

Forestier, H. and G. Rouger, "En marge de 'Monsieur Nicolas'; documents d'histoire sociale," *Annales de Bourgogne*, Vol. 10 (1938), pp. 198–213. Used documents to verify facts about Restif's early life.

Funck-Brentano, Frantz, "Rétif de la Bretonne, professeur d'histoire à Moulins," *Revue des études historiques*, année 77 (1911), pp. 589–594. Documents from the department of l'Allier, relating to Restif's prize chair in History.

Gentz, Dr. M., "Rétif de la Bretonne et la médicine," *Le Progrès Médical*, Vol. II (July, 1928), pp. 4–7.

Girault, Eusèble, "Analyse raisonnée des principaux ouvrages de Restif de la Bretonne," *La Revue des Romans*, II (1839), pp. 199–204.

Grubbs, H. A., "Further Light on the 'Dernière aventure' of Rétif de la Bretonne," *Modern Language Notes*, No. 66 (March, 1951), pp. 151–155. Prints a section of *Mes inscriptions* from newly found manuscripts.

Guégan, Bertrand, "Restif de la Bretonne apprenti, prote et imprimeur," *Arts et métiers graphiques*, année 8 (1934), pp. 29–36. Restif as printer.

Guillot, Gèrard, "Restif de la Bretonne par et pour les femmes," *Europe*, Nos. 427, 428 (1964), pp. 56–65. Calls Restif one of the most generous feminists of the 18th century.

Heine, Maurice, "Rétif de la Bretonne, et la femme féique," *Minotaure*, No. 6 (1935), pp. 53–56. Shows some prints from *Figures du Paysan perverti* by Binet.

———, "La Vieillesse de Restif de la Bretonne," *Hippocrate*, No. 7 (Sept., 1934), pp. 605–633. Asserts that Restif's fetishism was transformed, in old age, into a strong incest wish.

Hue, Gustave, "La famille de Restif de la Bretonne," *Mercure de France*, Vol. 85 (1910), pp. 206–227. He is on Restif's side against his wife Agnès.

Houville, G. d', "Au musée Carnavalet: Paris au XVIIIe siècle," *Revue des Deux Mondes*, No. 25 (Jan. 15, 1935), pp. 429–434. A chatty piece, reviewing the literary judgments on Restif.

Ioannisiani, A. R., "Restif de la Bretonne et le communisme utopique," *La Pensée*, March–April, 1958, pp. 99–103. This is a translation, slightly abridged, of an article appearing in the Russian journal *Questions d'histoire*, "A propos de l'histoire des idées du communisme utopique en France dans la période du Directoire," 1957. Basically, the argument is this: "It is incontestable that the general tendencies expressed in Restif's [autobiography] concur with the characteristic aspirations of the representatives of the intellectual democrats grouped around Babeuf." (p. 100)

———, "L'Utopie de Restif de la Bretonne," *Bulletin de l'Académie des Sciences de l'U.R.S.S.*, 7 série (1931), pp. 171–200, 833–856. This article is in Russian.

Lely, Gilbert, "Le Marquis de Sade et Rétif de la Bretonne," *Mercure de France*, No. 1130 (1957), pp. 364–366. Shows their mutual disdain.

Leroux, Pierre, "Lettres sur le Fouriérisme: Rétif de la Bretonne," *Revue Sociale*, March, 1950, pp. 103–107. Sees Fourier following Restif by "playing in a region halfway between the serious and the fantastic."

Louis, Dr., "Un Romancier fétichiste: Restif de la Bretonne," *Chronique Médicale*, année 11 (June 1, 1904), pp. 353–357. Uses *Le Joli Pied* to prove that Restif was a fetishist.

Louys, Pierre, "Un Roman inédit de Restif," *Revue des livres anciens*, tome I, 1913, pp. 87–94. The fragments from *L'Enclos et les oiseaux*.

Maynial, Edouard, "Les Mémoires de Casanova et les conteurs de XVIIIe siècle," *Mercure de France*, Vol. 103 (Jan. 1, 1928), pp. 112–137. Restif is closer to Casanova than anyone else in the 18th century. They both saw love as unattainable in its essence.

Pinset, Jacques, "Les Origines instinctives de la révolution française," *Revue d'histoire économique et sociale*, année 39 (1961), pp. 198–228. Uses Restif for a sociopsychological explanation for the violence of the masses in 1789.

Porter, Charles, "Imperiled Pedestrian," *Yale French Studies*, No. 32 (1964), pp. 55–67. Restif was attracted to Paris by its dangerous pleasures."

———, "Restif, Rousseau and Monsieur Nicolas," *Romantic Review*, No. 54, (Dec., 1963), pp. 262–273. Asserts that the "graphes" show a strong influence from Rousseau.

Pringault, F., "Restif de la Bretonne communiste," *Mercure de France*, tome 106 (Dec. 16, 1913), pp. 732–739. Claims that all of Fourier is in Restif.

Puychevrier, Sylvain, "Documents inédits sur Restif de la Bretonne," *Bulletin du Bouquiniste*, année 8 (1864).

Rouger, Gilbert, "L'Imprimerie Fournier et le séjour de Rétif à Auxerre," *Bulletin de la Société des sciences historiques et naturelle de l'Yonne*, année 82 (1928), pp. 207–221. Research was done at the local archives.

———, "Rétif auxerrois," *Annales de Bourgogne*, Vol. II (1930), pp. 56–69. Tests the veracity of Restif on his life at Auxerre.

Terrier, Max, "Rétif de la Bretonne," *Renaissance*, année 17 (1934), pp. 223–227. A discussion of the Carnavalet exhibition.

Terson, Dr. A., "Quelques remarques de Rétif sur le médecin, le chirurgien et l'oculiste," *Progrès Médical*, Vol. II (1935), pp. 1–4 of the supplement. Asserts the prescience of Restif's comments on the profession of medicine.

Thérive, André, "Restif de La Bretonne," *Ecrits de Paris*, No. 92 (1961), pp. 120–127. Looks at the novels as social history; finds the utopias absurd.

Thièbaut, Marcel, "Restif à Carnavalet," *Revue de Paris*, année 42 (1935), pp. 433–456. Criticizes the exhibit for omitting Restif's reform ideas.

———, "Restif ou Paris dévoilé," *Revue de Paris*, année 66 (1959), pp. 140–153. A favorable review of Chadourne's biography.

Tuzet, Hélène, "Deuz types de cosmogonies vitalistes: Restif de la Bretonne ou le coeur humain dévoilé," *Revue de sciences humaines*, Fasc. 100 (1960), pp. 495–506. Describes his cosmology as a vast, vitalistic dream, a resurrection of an astral religion.

Vallery-Radot, R., "Restif de la Bretonne réformateur et précurseur," *Revue Bleue*, année 27 (July 5, 1890), pp. 3–8.

Van Tichelen, H., "Restif de la Bretonne," *Vlaamse Gids*, Vol. 47 (1963), pp. 573–576. Written in Dutch.

[Villeterque, L. de], "Article nécrologique sur Restif de la Bretonne," *Journal de Paris*, Feb. 9, 1806, pp. 294–295. The eulogy calls Restif a writer "without style, but not without interest."

Weiss, "Notice biographique," *Biographie universelle de Michaud*, Vol. 37 (1827), pp. 391–397. Calls the utopias unworthy of study.

General Works

Bloch, Iwan, *Le Marquis de Sade et son temps*, trans. by A. Weber-Riga (Paris: Michalon, 1901).

Cabanès, Auguste, *Grands névropathes, malades immortels* (Paris: Michel, 1930–1935), 3 vols. See Vol. 2, pp. 71–96. He established the neurotic syndrome used by most other doctors writing on Restif.

Chinard, Gilbert, *L'Amérique et le rêve exotique dans la littérature française au XVIIIe siècle* (Paris: Hachette, 1913). Contains a chapter on travel literature in the lost half of the 18th century.

Crocker, Leslie, *Nature and Culture: Ethical Thought in the French Enlightenment* (Baltimore: Johns Hopkins, 1963).

Ellis, Havelock, *From Rousseau to Proust* (Boston: Houghton Mifflin, 1935). Judges Restif's thought as half genius, half platitude.

Flake, Otto, *Marquis de Sade, mit einem anhang über Rétif de La Bretonne* (Berlin: Fischer, 1930).

Green, F. C., *Minuet: A Critical Survey of French and English Literary Ideas in the Eighteenth Century* (London: Dent, 1935). Restif is precursor of Balzac, not a follower of Richardson.

Guilly, Paul, *Découverte de l'Ile Saint-Louis* (Paris: Michel, 1953). Restif conquered time by inscriptions.

Hassler, Karl, *Ludwig Tiecks Jugendroman, William Lovell und der Paysan perverti des Restif de la Bretonne* (Griefswald: J. Abel, 1902). A Germanic, detailed textual comparison of different editions.

Henriot, Emile, *Les Livres du second rayon, irréguliers et libertins* (Paris: Le Livre, 1925). See pp. 275–288. Restif here is still too vulgar for French taste.

Le Breton, André, *Le Roman au XVIIIe siècle* (Paris: Lecène and Oudin, 1898). See pp. 337–354 for Restif interpreted as a Rousseauian.

Lichtenberger, André, *Le Socialisme au XVIIIe siècle dans les écrivains français* (Paris, Alcan, 1895). Deals with Restif's ideas of property and equality, and calls him an important precursor of socialism.

Manuel, Frank and Fritzie, *French Utopias: An Anthology of Ideal Societies* (New York: Free Press, 1966). His translations from Restif's utopian writings.

Mauzi, Robert, *L'Idée du bonheur au XVIIIe siècle* (Paris: Colin, 1965).

Monselet, Charles, *Oubliés et dédaignés* (Paris: Bachelin-Deflorenne, 1885).

Nerval, Gérard de, *Les Illuminées, ou les Précurseurs du socialisme* (Paris: Champion, 1929). See especially "Restif communiste," pp. 270–280.

Palache, John Garber, *Four Novelists of the Old Regime* (London: J. Cape, 1926). Accepts too much of *Monsieur Nicolas* at face value.

Planhol, René de, *Les Utopistes de l'amour* (Paris: Garnier frères, 1921). Connects Restif with de Sade and Laclos.

Ruyer, Raymond, *L'Utopie et les utopies* (Paris: Presses universitaires de France, 1950). Discusses each of Restif's major utopian writings.

Saintsbury, George, *A History of the French Novel* (London: Macmillan, 1917), 2 vols. An early attempt to introduce Restif to England.

Viatte, Auguste, *Les Sources occultes du romantisme* (Paris: Champion, 1928).

Index

151